EFFECTIVE SPEECH COMMUNICATION in LEADING WORSHIP

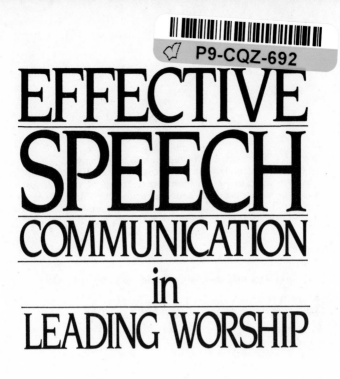

Charles L. Bartow

ABINGDON PRESS
Nashville

EFFECTIVE SPEECH COMMUNICATION IN LEADING WORSHIP

This book is printed on acid-free paper.

Library of Congress Cataloging-in-Publication Data

Bartow, Charles L.
   Effective speech communication in leading worship.

   Bibliography: p.
   Includes index.
   1. Public worship.   2. Oral communication.
   3. Reading in public worship.   I. Title.
BV15.B37   1988   251'.03   87-30622

ISBN 0-687-11533-7 (pbk. : alk. paper)

Scripture quotations except where noted are from the Revised Standard
Version of the Bible, copyrighted 1946, 1952, © 1971, 1973 by the Division of
Christian Education of the National Council of the Churches of Christ in the
U.S.A., and are used by permission.

"The Great Prayer of Thanksgiving" on pp. 118-19 is from *The Service for the
Lord's Day* (Supplemental Liturgical Resource 1). Copyright © 1984 the
Westminster Press. Used by permission. (This material is adapted and
revised from the earlier Westminster publication, *The Worshipbook—Services,*
1970. It includes material written by ICET.)

MANUFACTURED BY THE PARTHENON PRESS AT
NASHVILLE, TENNESSEE, UNITED STATES OF AMERICA

EFFECTIVE SPEECH COMMUNICATION
IN LEADING WORSHIP

WITH DEEP GRATITUDE

TO

W. J. BEENERS,

MENTOR, COLLEAGUE, FRIEND

CONTENTS

Introduction...9

1. The Dialogue of the Sanctuary.. 14

2. Speech Communication Dynamics in Leading Worship.... 23

3. Basic Considerations in Speaking the Written Word:
   Phrasing... 32

4. Basic Considerations in Speaking the Written Word:
   Emphasis..42

5. Speaking Calls to Worship and Benedictions.......................55

6. Leading Unison Confession and Responsive Praise...........67

7. Reading the Scriptures: Theory and Practice....................85

8. Administering Baptism and Serving Communion............ 108

   Bibliography.. 125

   Index.. 127

INTRODUCTION

Tis book is for anyone, seminary student, pastor, or layperson, who wishes to increase his or her understanding of what leadership in worship entails. I suppose the book is a "how to" for the most part. Certainly it is concerned with technique, with the art of skillful speech communication in worship. But technique is not just a matter of getting control of the voice and body so that they obey the mind. Technique is itself an affair of the mind. Before it is a way of doing anything, it is a way of thinking, of being.

Technique in speech communication is the way we put all that we are and can be into the service of content and purpose. It is not self-indulgence. It is not mere self-expression. It is rather self-immersion. If one's speech communication technique is sound, oneself is claimed by its task, is devoted to its task, is disciplined for its task.

This book is intended to help you and me grasp what is required of us if we are to speak responsibly from the lectern, pulpit, communion table, or baptismal font in church. We all are already competent in everyday speech. We know something of how to listen to people and respond to them. We know how to win a hearing for ourselves so that we can get on with our business. We have become sensitive to how we come across to others in all sorts of settings: in the thick of family play or quibbling, at the dinner table, at work, in public, and in private and intimate circumstances.

In all likelihood, however, we have not had any experience that has directly prepared us to lead in worship, for worship is not just an everyday affair. It is something special. It is a time set apart to gather as a community of sisters and brothers in Christ, to call to mind what God has done among us throughout our history. Worship focuses our attention on God and the difference God makes for those who believe that life is to be lived in fellowship with the divine. How does one speak in such a Presence? How does one speak *to* such a Presence? How does one lead others in the worship of the One who is present with each of us and all of us together in ways that go clean beyond our capacity to comprehend? Those questions are not just questions of theology—though they are that. They are questions of speech communication technique, too. Throughout this book, therefore, those questions are explored from a number of different angles.

I have tried to write the book so that it may be useful to people of various Christian traditions. Therefore, I have distinguished between what I call speech communication principles and the way those principles are executed in any particular case. For example, one of the principles I discuss in relation to serving communion is that the word needs to be suited to the action and the action to the word. What that means to a Roman Catholic, Presbyterian, Wesleyan, or Baptist, however, may be something quite different. Each would need to suit action to word and word to action in a way consonant with his or her best understanding of what was going on, say, in the blessing of the bread and cup and in offering the communion elements to the people.

In illustrating the execution of principles, I have had to rely on my own reading and experience and the knowledge and experience shared with me by others. Those others represent a wide array of worship traditions. My own tradition is Presbyterian-Reformed. What I have come to understand best and to feel most at home articulating consequently reflects that Presbyterian-Reformed heritage. Where the reader finds that heritage limiting my understanding too severely, I beg for charity. Yet more and more I have come to believe that unique points of view shared in the marketplace of ideas yield much that is capable of generalization. So it is my hope that from the particulars presented here, you will be able to educe something of use to yourself and others. That is to say, although the principles of effective speech communication may have universal value, I hope that many, if not most, of the illustrations and exercises given in these pages will also be adaptable for use in a variety of worship traditions.

Effective Speech Communication in Leading Worship is intended to be both a textbook and a workbook. That is, it gives something to you by way of information and theory. But it expects something from you, too, by way of practice and critical reflection on practice. I have found over the years that the most difficult part of any speech communication task is not in failing to get an idea of what needs to be done. The most difficult part is doing it, accurately assessing what was done, and modifying one's speech behavior to bring it more into line with intention.

Speech communication in worship or anywhere else is highly subjective. It is "I-thou," not "I-it" stuff. As a result, there is threat as well as promise when one steps into the chancel of a church sanctuary to lead in the worship of God. There is the threat of exposure. Someone—maybe everyone—can catch a glimpse of the kind of person I actually am, and that person may wonder, *Why do the words of that psalm offend him? Why is he reluctant to throw himself into that bouyant call to worship or ringing declaration of faith?* Yet suppose I do invest myself fully in something that at first I find intimidating. Might I not then discover something about myself that I like, something about others that I like, something about God that I never knew before? Who can tell?

There is risk in reach! Yet there is risk in not reaching as well. There is danger in never trying. One can worry oneself into a smaller and smaller view of self, of others, of God. Certainly there can be moments of failure in worship leadership, but there can be moments of exhilaration also. By the grace of God we can learn from them all, profit from them all, grow through them all. Inevitably we will become quite aware of those areas where we need more work, more refinement of technique. We will become aware of possibilities in speech communication in worship we were unaware of before. And we will become conscious of the need constantly to evaluate what we are about and the way we go about it. The trick, as my colleague Karl Light put it a number of years ago, is to become conscious of self, but not self-conscious. We can do it if the *focus* of our attention is in the right place: not upon self, but task; not upon threat, but promise.

I have not tried to cover everything that could be covered in a textbook-workbook on effective speech communication in leading worship. On the other hand, I have tried to cover those tasks that present the reader with representative problems and possibilities in leading worship. The book will prove more useful, I think, if chapters 1 through 4 are read first. The remaining chapters may be read in any order according to the felt needs of the individual reader. I have also attempted to write the book so that it can be used in workshop settings. It can serve as a supplementary text in a seminary class on worship and worship leadership. It can serve as the textbook for a practicum on leadership in worship. It can be used in lay-leader workshops conducted in local churches. Particularly, I think the chapters dealing with responsive readings from the psalter, and theory and practice in the reading of the Scriptures should prove beneficial to the laity and to the clergy alike. The chapter on administering baptism and serving communion (8), however, is aimed chiefly at the ordained clergy and those studying in seminary with a view to ordination.

There are no footnotes, although credit is given in the text to those from whom particular insights have been borrowed. A good deal of research, especially in the technical areas of speech, voice and diction, kinesics, and the oral interpretation of literature, undergirds what is offered in these pages, but the book is not a research tool. Therefore, research is not given prominence. The bibliography also is limited exclusively to those works that might enhance further reflection and practice in relation to the principles delineated here. It is not a full bibliography of sources, nor is it representative of the scope of reading required of the one wishing to develop a full knowledge of the theology and practice of worship. To fill that kind of need, numerous additional scholarly publications are available and should be consulted.

I want to thank a number of persons who have contributed directly to my writing. The staff at Abingdon Press have been most helpful and encouraging in their work with me. Cullen I. K. Story, Associate Professor of New Testament, Emeritus, of Princeton Theological Seminary, consulted with me concerning some technical matters in the section of chapter 6 dealing with responsive praise. Howard Rice, Professor of Ministry at San Francisco Theological Seminary, read every chapter and provided wise, substantive critique. My wife, Paula—may her name be praised in the gates!—typed the entire manuscript and did a large part of the hard work of proofreading. My students at San Francisco Theological Seminary have challenged me and taught me much through their participation in basic speech classes and the class, "Worship in the Reformed-Presbyterian Tradition," which I co-teach with Howard Rice. Further, San Francisco Theological Seminary itself has a generous sabbatic leave policy, which made it possible for me to escape the everyday demands of instruction long enough to do the writing. So to the seminary I must give a word of thanks. Then, too, I want to thank my mother-in-law, Ruth M. Goetschius, who provided housing and meals for me and my family during my sabbatic leave. She has done us a great service. I especially appreciate the large, second-story room she turned over to me with its view of trees and lawn and with its large desk, bookcase, and peace and quiet: a sabbatic leave's dream! But above all I want to thank the man to whom this book is dedicated, W. J. Beeners, Carl and Helen Egner Professor of Speech at Princeton Theological Seminary. His class "The Spoken Word in Worship" inspired this book, and what Dr. Beeners has been teaching at Princeton for nearly forty years has provided much of its substance. Indeed, I think it true to say that the book could not have been written without him.

Ramsey, New Jersey
February 28, 1987

CHAPTER ONE

THE DIALOGUE OF THE SANCTUARY

Before talking about *effective* speech communication in
leading worship, it is important that we come to some
mutual understanding of worship from a *speech
communication* point of view. As I am using the term, *effective
speech communication* means the capacity to speak and act
appropriately. Leading worship requires that we express
ourselves in a manner appropriate to the occasion, something we plainly cannot do if we do not have at least a
preliminary idea of what the occasion is.

This first chapter, therefore, discusses the nature of
worship. Following that, I describe the shape of worship and
what factors need to be considered when one is leading
worship. The remaining chapters are devoted to treating
selected portions of the service of worship. None of the
discussions are exhaustive or definitive. Rather they are
suggestive. It is hoped that you, the reader, will feel free to
take from them what is useful for your own purposes.
Expand them where that is warranted. Modify them to meet
the requirements of your particular tradition. Criticize them
in the light of your theological convictions and adapt them to
meet whatever needs are pressing in your own local setting.

There are essentially two ways to look at an experience to
achieve an understanding of it. One way is to stand apart,
using tools of observation and critique in order to describe
the experience in ways others, using the same tools, would
also describe it. So the social scientist can take a hard look at a
service of worship and describe what people do, how they do
it, who leads, who follows, and how what is done appears to
be related to the society and culture in which the service of
worship takes place. Likewise a specialist in liturgics (the
theory and practice of worship), can use historical and
theological norms to determine to what extent the worship of

a given community appears to be ordered and conducted in a manner consonant with traditional expectations. For example, if the worship being observed is supposed to be representative of those traditions favoring an entirely free hand for local pastors and people in determining the form and content of services of worship, you do not expect to find prescribed prayers spoken each Lord's day, lectionary readings of Scripture scrupulously followed week after week, and holy communion celebrated every Sunday year in and year out. In fact, a so-called "free church" congregation's worship, no doubt, would be regarded as highly irregular if it followed a pattern such as the one just described. On the other hand, it would be deemed highly irregular if a Roman or Anglo-Catholic church did not follow such a pattern.

Those kinds of observations and conclusions are not really debatable. They are generally recognized as valid. They provide us information needed to understand and assess the conduct of worship with reference to traditional settings and sociocultural circumstances. Their usefulness is a function of their accuracy.

Another way to look at the experience of worship is as a participating subject whose observations are not universally shared, whose tools of analysis are unique to his or her own perspective and purpose, and whose assertions, as a result, are thoroughly debatable. Such is the way I now ask you to look at worship with me.

Some accurate and useful information may be provided in what I have to say. I hope so! My real goal, however, is to get you to think with me about worship as an experience in which people listen to and talk with God and one another. If we can achieve at least a tentative meeting of minds on that score, perhaps we can then move ahead to explore options for doing our listening and talking with ever increasing competence and integrity. What we will end up with, God willing, are insights to be reflected on and not conclusions to be defended, principles to be put into use, not rules to be obeyed.

When it comes to leading worship, nobody has all the answers, nobody is sufficiently expert, for worship involves us in the deepest mysteries of faith and life, God and humanity. Technical considerations of speech communication theory are important, and theological astuteness is something we should strive for, but none of that guarantees a thing. We give God and one another our best efforts. What else have we that is worth giving? However, God alone can provide what our best efforts can never achieve, assurance of the divine Presence in judgment and mercy. In all our thinking about worship, our participation in worship, our leading of worship, if we are wise, we pray for that.

Worship is work. It is *our* work, but it is our work undertaken in the light of what God has done and is continuing to do in and among us through Jesus Christ. The *first* thing that needs to be affirmed about the nature of worship, therefore, is this: It needs to be understood always as involving the divine initative and human response.

We are not the first persons in the world to contend with that divine initiative and to frame a suitable human response, however. No, the issue of how to respond to God's self-disclosure has been there from the beginning with Sarah and Abraham and their descendants, for example, and with Jesus, his disciples, and their descendants up to and including you and me. It is in the biblical record and through the witness of the church over time that we receive direction for our own work and witness, mission and worship. Thus, the real danger of bland, unimaginative, repetitive worship, it seems to me, springs not from a fear of experimentation. Generally we have plenty of that. I think it springs instead from a loss of historical sense, a failure to care about the links with the past that may disclose to us something of how God's future may be breaking in on us in the present. How could we ever discover that God chooses such unlikely candidates as Egyptian slaves, exiles, refugees, sinners, and the Friend of sinners (Luke 7:34) to manifest the divine rule, the familial fellowship of the kingdom of God, except through the Scriptures and through the worship of the church in which the Scriptures are read and preached? And how could we discover what it costs us to enlist in the vanguard of God's future, except as we participate in representing Christ's own passion—the celebration of the holy eucharist or communion—and there receive the sustenance we need to carry on in the face of the world's "no" to God?

In a word, how could we know what it means to take up a cross and follow Christ except as we see what it has meant? As a preacher I once heard put it, the degradations of our pornography, the rattling of our armaments, and the inanities of our advertising do not present us with exhibit one of an emerging nobility. The question we need to ask ourselves as we contemplate what to do in worship, therefore, is not, Is this "old hat" or is this novel? Instead, our question should be, Is this profoundly resonant with the gospel that has been turning the world upside down age upon age? The *second* thing that needs to be affirmed about the nature of worship, then, is this: It needs to be understood always as involving a disciplined innovation coupled with a responsible reclamation of the past.

Even in our present time and in our particular denominations and congregations, however, we cannot link innovation and tradition responsibly all on our own. We need one another. We need the church ecumenical, the worldwide church of all times *and* places. Worship not only has a history, it has a rich and diverse contemporary practice. Nor should that rich and varied practice be ignored, unless, of course, we want to be cut off from our sisters and brothers in Christ in order to get on with our "own thing." That *is* an option!

However, it is the ecumenical church that has provided us with our Bible. It is the ecumenical church that has provided us with our hymnody. The Roman Catholic Church sings Lutheran hymns. The Presbyterians sing the songs of Charles and John Wesley. Black Christians—Baptists, Roman Catholics, Reformed, and others—have given us their liberation music, the spirituals, without which all denominations would be impoverished musically, liturgically, theologically. In the hymnbook you find the poetry of women, of men, of ethnic minority and majority persons, of Europeans and Asians, Russians and Americans. And we have still to mention medieval plainsong, the Renaissance anthems, and today's works, which give wings to our worship.

But our worship, though owing more to the ecumenical

church than can be calculated, is also a very local, hometown thing. The battered pewter communion bread plate sitting there on that table in the old stone country sanctuary is not just a liturgical relic. It is a valued symbol to every member of the congregation in that place. It reminds each of the congregation's members of the generations that have gone before, all of them part of the communion of saints. In ordering worship and leading it, such symbols, as well as local customs and the expectations associated with the liturgical traditions we are a part of, need to be given their place along with the variety of ecumenical contributions.

A service that is all local color obviously could degenerate into a clubby activity, something inhospitable to the stranger and thus a contradiction of the gospel. Then too, a service of worship that is vaguely ecumenical, that tries to be all things to all people, could degenerate into a chaotic, vague, impersonal experience nobody truly feels a part of. The task, therefore, is to maintain a sane balance between universality and particularity, between ecumenical consensus and variety on the one hand, and congregational and traditional distinctiveness on the other. Thus, a *third* thing can be affirmed about the nature of worship, specifically this: Worship needs to be understood always as involving a tasteful and theologically defensible integration of ecumenical awareness with traditional, congregational uniqueness.

Worship is also both a public-corporate experience and an experience of profound personal significance. In the setting of our worship of God, we are not to think of ourselves simply as a collection of individuals who have our primary social identity determined elsewhere. Instead, we are to think of ourselves as a unique people created out of a diversity of cultural, economic, racial, and family backgrounds by the Christ who has conscripted us into the service of the Kingdom about which he preached.

Christ's identity itself is determined in the realm of service to that Kingdom. He is the eternal Son of his heavenly Parent, true, but he is also, at the same time, the firstborn of many brothers and sisters (Rom. 8:29). To be the only begotten Child of divinity, to be the Christ of God, is not to be a lonely religious talent strutting before a disbelieving world, but a Friend of sinners (Luke 7:34) building a new family for humankind out of the scattered and contentious peoples of the earth. The meek among us, the outcasts, the despised, the oppressed, the poor, the lonely, the ill, and the ill-clad may be the first to come into that family, for they perhaps have no illusions concerning the probability of a true and lasting familial welcome elsewhere. The family home, however, is open to all who will enter it now and eternally. Jesus said, "In my Father's house are many rooms" (John 14:2). No one need be excluded.

In worship we celebrate our inclusion in Christ's family. We celebrate the fact that we ourselves are in Christ doing what he calls us to do, suffering what he calls us to suffer—the ambiguity of living in a world that, as a rule, appears to want no part of the future God intends for it. In worship we know ourselves as meant for cross-bearing, for peace making, for doing justice. We meet together in Christ—our true sanctuary—as adoptive children of our heavenly Parent. That's the way the apostle Paul saw it. And as adoptive children of the divine Parent, "Joint heirs of Christ" (Rom. 8:17 kjv), we bear the word and do the work of the Kingdom.

We may bear that word and do that work fitfully, at times halfheartedly. After all, when we worship God, we also confess our sins, our betrayals, our failures in *noblesse oblige*. But we still bear the word of the Kingdom and do its work. We are not a complete failure either together or individually. That's the crux of the matter for us. God will not have our failure forever, nor will God let us hang on to it. In Christ there is absolution of sin, of our falling short of the mark. So we go on, our compromised deeds shining in the radiant fidelity of the Christ, our stammering witness made eloquent by his speech, "Father, forgive them; for they know not what they do" (Luke 23:34). That is the ground for determining personal identity and for understanding one's private experience in public worship.

What happens in worship is first of all a corporate, public experience, yet obviously something also takes place within each of us as individual human beings. We deal with our own call to service in the Kingdom. We know the responsibilities of sisterhood and brotherhood in Christ as personal responsibilities. We assess our own failures. And we hear Christ Jesus' words of forgiveness, restitution, and new beginning as intended not just for somebody else or for the church as a whole, but for us. Christ our Savior is Christ *your* Savior and *mine*. The *fourth* and final thing to be affirmed about the nature of worship then, is as follows: Worship needs to be understood always as a corporate-public experience shared by individual human beings at the very depths of personal consciousness.

A word that may suffice to characterize the experience of worship as I have just described it is *tensiveness*. In speech communication theory, particularly that portion of it having to do with the oral reading of literature, tensiveness refers to the creative stresses and strains one is subjected to in the attempt to give voice and body to a discourse. A piece of literature, for example, does not "come alive" for us except as we enter into the give and take of its world. For illustration, look at Psalm 27. If the psalm is to "come alive" for us, we will have to find a way to state its apparently contradictory thoughts from the standpoint of a single human being at prayer. The psalmist, you will recall, begins by saying:

> The Lord is my light and my salvation;
> whom shall I fear?
> The Lord is the stronghold of my life;
> of whom shall I be afraid?
>
> (27:1)

At about midpoint in the psalm, however, we hear these words:

> Hear, O Lord, when I cry aloud,
> be gracious to me and answer me!
>
> (27:7)

Suddenly it becomes clear to us that the psalmist is not just making a stouthearted affirmation concerning God, but is also imploring God to be light, salvation, and a stronghold in the midst of deep need, loneliness, danger. Consequently, as readers of the psalm, we must share in its desperation if we are to share in its hope. We must express its utter anguish if we are truly to hear and believe what it affirms. Reduce the psalm to unmitigated praise and you so distort it as nearly to end its life. Make of the psalm nothing but a litany of anxious petition and you do the same, for the psalm lives in the experience of its contradictions. It speaks only by way of a voice fraught with tensiveness.

Worship speaks with a voice fraught with tensiveness. There is the divine initiative and human response. There is tradition and innovation. There is universality and particularity. Worship has a public, corporate character, yet it holds at the same time, intensely personal, even private significance for us. And like the psalm we have just been discussing, its praise is rarely unmixed with petition. Its affirmation is hardly ever untouched by confession. In the experience of worship, we may thrill to the glory of God, but always that glory casts upon the earth the shadow of a cross.

To speak effectively in leading worship, therefore, means that we must never lose touch with that tensiveness. We will talk of God, but always with our humanity intact. We will dare to speak our own minds, but only to the extent that we are also willing to hear the witness of the Scriptures and the church concerning the mind of Christ. We will strive to be responsive to those gathered before us, yet at the same time we will attempt to keep ourselves and those before us responsive to the needs of the wider church and world. We will take one another seriously as individuals, but we will not turn the dialogue of the sanctuary into a chat with "our kind of people." Instead, we will stay cognizant of the fact that what people, *all* people, are to become is God's people in Christ. The corporate, public character of our identity and worship, that is to say, will not be compromised in an attempt at mere homey intimacy.

As was said near the beginning of this chapter, worship is an experience in which we listen to and talk with God and one another. Effective speech-communication in leading worship, speech-communication that is appropriate to its worship setting, will keep that in mind. The dialogue of the sanctuary is never easy, is never casual, for it is by nature full of tensiveness. Tensiveness, however, is not bane, but blessing. It is a tautness that lets the soul sing.

CHAPTER TWO

SPEECH COMMUNICATION
DYNAMICS IN LEADING WORSHIP

The experience of worship is characterized by tensiveness, a tautness that is the result of holding together in
silence, speech, and action the contrasting elements
that define the nature of worship. Those contrasting
elements are the divine initiative and human response,
tradition and innovation, universality and particularity, and
corporate and personal participation. Eliminate one element
or another, and you do not strengthen worship; you weaken
it. Remove all the tensiveness, and you do not make worship
more simple, calm, peaceful, soothing, and agreeable, you
make it deadly. Worship without tensiveness ends with the
sterile uniformity of polite smiles.

It is possible to be "underwhelmed" even in the presence of
God. It is possible to be "underwhelming." We may have it all
right in principle and on paper: an order of worship that makes
sense given our historical and theological commitments,
profound passages of Scripture identified for public reading,
the offering of cash, praise, and prayer each set in its rightful
place, hymns chosen and at hand in our hymnbooks, the
sacrament of holy communion properly prepared, a final
blessing ready to be given and received. But a service of
worship does not take place on paper or in principle. It takes
place in space and time, in those who lead and in those who
follow, in the choir and in the congregation, in you and in me.

The tensiveness of the service of worship is not something
that can be known and felt on paper and in principle. It is
something that can be known and felt only when what is
understood in principle and laid out on paper gets spoken,
heard, and done. The music of Mozart is known and felt
when the notes of the score are played. The poetry of
Browning and the plays of Shakespeare live in performance.
Stories come to life when we read or tell them. Likewise,

23

worship happens when we do it. The divine initiative and human response, the tradition and innovation, the universality and particularity, the corporateness and the more personal qualities of worship are experienced in the coming together of pastors and people, lay liturgists and worshipers. They are known as the Scriptures are read and heard, as the sermon is preached and listened to, as the sacraments are offered and received, as prayers are articulated, silently or aloud, and as affirmations of faith are made.

In a very real sense, worship is a drama, an act, a deed of creation and re-creation. It is not make believe, yet it involves what drama characteristically involves: plot, character, setting, a beginning, middle, and end. It calls for empathy, for imaginative participation in experiences that are not precisely one's own. After all, there is *anamnesis* in worship. There is living memorialization of God's liberating people from oppression and sin in Egypt and Babylon, Jerusalem and Rome. Above all else there is remembrance of the sacrifice of Christ as we present our souls and bodies as a "living sacrifice," an oblation or thank offering, "holy and acceptable to God," fit for the accomplishment of liberating deeds today, "which is [our] spiritual worship" (Rom. 12:1).

In a word, worship calls for *embodiment*, the service and praise of God in flesh and blood and muscle. The women, men, and children in the pews are not just spectators at a divine happening. To the contrary, by the Spirit, they are the evidence of God's initiative still being exercised in the affairs of peoples and nations. They are present at God's behest to do God's work and to share God's glory. At least in this sense, worship is their responsibility, and it is the task of leaders in worship to see to it that they are aided and encouraged in exercising their responsibility. As the Christ of God was not a lonely religious talent strutting before a disbelieving world, so those who lead in worship are not virtuoso performers seeking the acclaim of admiring congregations. They lead in the *service* of worship. They help the congregation in the moment of worship to be and to do what it is called to be and to do.

That means, for example, that if the congregation is to hear the word of God as the Scriptures are read, leaders in worship will have to do that hearing *with* the congregation. They will have to become listeners who speak to facilitate other people's listening. And if the congregation is to offer its life at the altar or at the table as a witness to what God is up to in the world, making the last first and the first last, bringing hope out of despair and life out of death, then those who lead in worship will have to be ready to use intellect, heart, will, voice, and body to help congregations see and understand what is required of them and what is promised to them.

The altar or table does not belong to the priest or pastor. Instead, both altar and table belong to the Christ who has invited all who will to come and receive the food of the Kingdom, sustenance for the work of the Kingdom. The leader's task, then, is to incarnate that hospitality, give voice to Christ's invitation, and anticipate the people's response. The leader offers bread and wine to the people, who then take what is offered and share it with one another.

The shape of the service of worship is thus a dramatic movement in time. It begins with God's calling people to be the people of God. It continues with God's formation of the people, through word and sacrament, as a divine possession, fit to bear witness to the kingdom of God in the midst of the world. It ends with the people of God going out into the world to be and to do what God has commanded, renewed in purpose and fortified with faith, hope, and love. To lead in a service of worship is to discern that shape or movement, to invest oneself in it, heart, mind, and will, and to speak and act in order that others may do the same.

Such investment of oneself in the drama of worship in order to share it with others through speech and action is what I refer to as the *interpretative dynamic* in leading worship. I use the word *dynamic*, because speech in worship is not in any way mechanical. It is not a matter of simply grasping with the intellect the plain sense of a call to worship or a prayer of confession and then stating it as if it had nothing to do with us personally. It has everything to do with us personally. It has everything to do with every person in the sanctuary, and all persons together. We need to "live into" what we speak. We need to be grasped by the intellectual and emotional content of the call or confession and to manifest at the same time, in words, vocal tone, posture, facial expression, and gesture what has grasped us.

A professor of the oral interpretation of literature once put it this way. He said we have to "outer" whatever we "inner." Further, we have to do both the "innering" and the "outering" in the very moment we speak. The speech act in leading worship, that is to say, requires of us that we be fully present and responsive to the given elements of the drama of worship. Stated as simply as I know how, we need to know what we are saying, we need to know why we are saying it, and we need to speak and act according to this knowledge. As a speech teacher of mine has said, "Expression must equal impression."

We also need to know to whom we are speaking when we lead worship and we need to be aware of the setting in which our worship takes place. Just as there is an interpretative dynamic operative when we conduct services of worship, so also there is a *situational dynamic*. We do not speak in a vacuum. We speak in a specific place, large or small, of ornate or simple appointment. In a tiny, rural sanctuary such as the one I myself led worship in for a number of years, to say "Our help is in the name of the Sovereign God who made heaven and earth," is one thing. To say the same words in Riverside Church in New York City or Grace Cathedral in San Francisco is something else entirely. Likewise, what may be a perfectly understandable gesture from the lectern or pulpit in the one place might seem to be nothing more than a tic or mannerism in the other. Obviously, in the larger setting, more size is required in one's gesturing and more intensity of support for one's voice is needed, along with an increase in volume, a lengthening of vowel sound and flow, and an energizing of the diction.

Always the object is to appear "natural" and "conversational" of course, but what appears natural and conversational in one worship space may appear utterly foolish and inappropriate elsewhere. A painting on my office wall, left to the department of speech communication and homiletics at San Francisco Theological Seminary by our former dean and professor of preaching, Browne Barr, shows a stern-faced preacher bellowing his thoughts from a wooden pulpit in a small church while some choir members talk, others sleep, and an elder sits helplessly by smiling politely through the obviously inappropriate and irrelevant harangue. The painting wins a guffaw from everyone who looks at it. The discrepancy between setting and manner of speech couldn't be more pronounced or ludicrous.

Yet it can also go the other way. It is possible to understate as well as to overstate. If we have all suffered from the overpowering presence of someone in the chancel of the sanctuary, we also have suffered from the very nearly real absence of the liturgist or worship leader. Both extremes are to be avoided. What is needed is a clear statement that, in a way suitable to the physical setting in which the service of worship takes place, discloses what the worship leader has to say and his or her purpose in saying it.

We do not only speak in a specific place when we lead worship, however. We also speak in a specific liturgical setting. Even before the call to worship gets spoken by us, for instance, something else doubtless has been going on. A prelude of one kind or another has been played. Perhaps an introit has been sung as well. What was the tone or mood of that prelude or introit? Was it bombastic, some thunderous rendition of a well-known hymn? Or was it quiet, reflective, prayerful? Was the tempo fast or slow? Were people paying attention to it? Were they in tune with it? Did it seem to go over their heads as they whispered greetings to one another while settling into their pews? Clearly one cannot get up to deliver a call to worship as if nothing has happened, as if no music has been played or sung, as if nobody has heard it or responded to it or ignored it. Throughout the entire service of worship, the appropriate handling of any particular element must be decided with alertness to what precedes and what is to follow.

Again, this is not a matter of mechanics, but of sensitivity. To be fully present in one's role as leader in worship is to be fully attentive to what is going on before, during, and after one speaks. Content and purpose are at the forefront of one's attention. They are the focus. But content cannot be fully expressed and one's purpose cannot be fully achieved if liturgical setting is overlooked. To pay no mind to liturgical setting, to fail to give heed to what has preceded one's own efforts and to what is going to follow, and to neglect congregational response is not to "stick to the subject" or to be laudably disinterested in the results of one's efforts. It is to be indifferent to those who are also contributing to leadership in worship, and it is to neglect the task of facilitating the liturgical work of the congregation. After all, the true objective or purpose in giving expression to anything is to enable others to perceive it in a way conducive to their full participation in the act of worship. The leader in worship is a servant of the Word to that end. One's purpose in worship leadership is achieved in relation to the gathered worshipers and appropriately to the liturgical setting or it is not achieved at all.

In summary, with regard to the interpretative dynamic in leading worship, it is the speaker's task to involve herself or himself in the intellectual and emotional content of the textual material being handled (call to worship, responsive psalter reading, Scripture reading, communion prayers), and to determine and identify with the material's implicit purpose. With regard to the situational dynamic, it is the speaker's task to express the intellectual and emotional content of the material being handled with sensitivity to what precedes and follows it in the order of worship and with alertness to expected and actual listener response. This is to be done in order that one's purpose in speaking may be achieved.

At this point it must be apparent that, as I see it, the role of the leader in worship is an assertive, not a passive one. The leader *leads*. The leader does not follow. She or he is not just part of the crowd. Furthermore, the leader leads by listening as well as by speaking. He or she attempts to hear the word that is to be spoken, whatever it is, from call to worship to benediction, and to speak that word so that others can hear it and respond.

To illustrate, let me return to the opening sentence of the traditional call to worship I quoted a page or two ago: "Our help is in the name of the Sovereign God who made heaven and earth." Surely the intended effect of a sentence such as that is not to provoke indifference to the presence and power of God in human life. Rather its intended effect is to evoke confident trust in God. The statement makes it clear that the one who is adequate to help us pursue the divine purpose in life is not some effete deity who can't be trusted to stick with it, but is in fact the creator of the ends of the earth and of the vastnesses of space. That God, by whom and for whom all things are made, is the God in whom "we live and move and have our being" (Acts 17:28).

We are called to worship that God, nothing other and nothing less. Assertive worship leaders should hear that call for themselves and speak what they hear so that others likewise can hear it. They should not speak as if God were the creator of an eighth-grade geography class globe. They should not speak as if God had no strength at all, as if God were timid, exhausted, ineffectual. And they should not speak as if divinity had no interest in human affairs, no concern for helping women and men who are hard pressed in the pursuit of holiness, peace, and justice. To the contrary, assertive worship leaders will stand tall and confident, look person to person into the eyes of the congregation gathered before them, and speak to that congregation in tones adequate to suggest that they know what they are talking about.

Or, to change the illustration and to deal with a text completely different from the one just quoted, if assertive worship leaders were reading the words of Psalm 27:7, "Hear, O Lord, when I cry aloud, be gracious to me and answer me!" they would not speak as if they thought the psalmist had no cause to plead with the divine or as if the psalmist were commanding rather than beseeching God. To the contrary, in body, face, and tone of voice they would attempt to suggest the psalmist's deep need as they understood it in their own minds and hearts. And they would express what they understood in order to assist the congregation in taking into its mind and heart the plight and cry of the psalmist.

Assertive worship leaders, therefore, do not call attention to themselves, for the self is not being asserted. Nor do assertive leaders set one prevailing mood or attitude suitable primarily to themselves and then accommodate every word spoken in worship to that basic mood or attitude. Instead, assertive worship leaders take the initiative in understanding what the word to be spoken is all about and what it requires by way of a worshiper's response. They then take the initiative in making that response. In other words, assertive worship leaders seek to engender what they have themselves come to believe, understand, and do as a result of grappling with the text or word they are called on to speak. Leadership in worship, in this sense, is not a matter of telling people what to do, though even that at times needs to be done. It is rather a matter of taking the lead in comprehending and doing what needs to be comprehended and done in each moment of worship so that all worshipers together may accomplish what is expected of them as a congregation. Leadership in worship, properly exercised, promotes congregational cohesiveness. Despite our diversities, and without denying them, it helps us to be and act as one.

No one, of course, is ever able to achieve a level of consummate skill in handling the interpretative and situational dynamics of speech communication in worship. There is simply too much that is unpredictable. We can never know what "works" for everyone. We cannot predict what each person in a congregation will make of what we say. Nor can we predetermine the response of the congregation as a whole. However, this imprecision and lack of control over people's reactions should not bother us much, for our goal is not to manipulate response, but to secure involvement.

Within the setting of the congregation's corporate worship, many personal and private experiences are occurring. The management of these is God's business, not ours, as indeed the management of any corporate, congregational experience in the end is God's business. We lead people in worship. We do not and cannot—and should not care to—dictate what significance it will hold for them. Just ask preachers, even those acknowledged to be among the most competent, about the varied hearings their sermons receive among listeners, and you will get some idea of just how free the Spirit of God can be in interpreting the word to people's hearts! Whatever our skill at our point of entry into this business of leading worship, however, we can further increase our ability to "outer" what we "inner." We can strive to match expression to impression. What effective speech communication in leading worship requires of us then is not a perfectionist attitude, but a willingness to experiment, to grow, and to extend the range and increase the precision of both our perception and expression of meaning. In the next chapter, we will start extending that range and increasing that precision as we attend to some very basic considerations in speaking the written word.

CHAPTER THREE

BASIC CONSIDERATIONS IN SPEAKING THE WRITTEN WORD: PHRASING

Surely it goes without saying that leading worship, for the most part, entails the speaking of written texts. From beginning to end, our services of worship make use of biblical and other written materials that need to be understood and communicated understandably. Calls to worship typically are sentences taken from Scripture and are meant to orient us, to give us our bearings as we come into the presence of God for purposes of worship. Corporate confession of sin, not consistently practiced in all Christian traditions, but clearly practiced quite regularly in many if not most, entails the unison reading of a printed text. Then there are prayers of other types, the Lord's Prayer and litanies, for example, and there are responsive or unison readings from the psalter, statements of faith such as the Apostles' Creed, Old Testament and New Testament lessons, and the benediction, which, like the call to worship, customarily consists of scriptural sentences or traditional formulas.

In successive chapters, these and other particular elements in the service of worship will be considered in detail. For the present, however, it is important to discuss what is basic to the responsible handling of them all. Our concern, that is to say, is with the elementals of the spoken word in worship, how to get at the sense of a printed text and speak it. We shall deal first with phrasing, grouping words into easily understood units of thought that tell one thing at a time. After that, we shall deal with emphasis, how to lift a word into prominence in order to arrest attention and to discriminate the important idea in a phrase from all related ideas.

As we begin these explanations and exercises, I want to stress something that I mentioned earlier, namely, that we are concerned here not with rules to be slavishly obeyed, but with principles to be creatively engaged. In speech communication, whether in worship or in any other situation, there are no techniques, no "how to do it" tips that will guarantee results. Instead, each person's soul, mind, and strength over and over again need to be given to the task of making sense of what is to be spoken. Therefore, we turn now to the task of perceiving and expressing the sense of selected, brief excerpts of scriptural texts in order to discern the principles involved in making sense. You will need to engage these principles on your own and in a way suitable to yourself when you lead in a service of worship.

As I have just said, the purpose of phrasing is to group words into easily understood units of thought that tell one thing at a time. However, no one should get the idea that such units of thought are static entities. If we look at units of thought as they are arranged on a page with commas, colons, semicolons, and periods, they may appear to be static, but as soon as we speak those thoughts, they come alive. Punctuation, in fact, cannot always be relied on as a clue to the spoken phrase. Sometimes a spoken phrase will go right through a comma. At other times it may halt momentarily where there is no comma. Thus, phrasing in speech communication, like phrasing in music, needs to be understood as a movement in time. Further, the significance of each spoken phrase needs to be determined by the contribution the phrase makes to the development of the complete sentence. In settling on the best way to phrase a passage, then, we need to decide how words should be grouped so that the progression of thought in the sentence as a whole may be discerned with relative ease by the listener. To state it as succinctly as possible, we need to ask ourselves what belongs with what.

Take, for example, this verse from the book of Hebrews: "Whoever would draw near to God must believe that he exists and that he rewards those who seek him" (Heb. 11:6). There is no comma anywhere in that sentence to tell you what belongs with what, yet it would be somewhat awkward to read through the passage with no break whatsoever. Not only would the listener very likely get the feeling of a run-on sentence from such delivery, but the speaker might run out of breath before the entire sentence was spoken! Nor does changing versions of the text necessarily help. In the King James Version, for instance, the sentence reads this way: "He that cometh to God must believe that he is, and that he is a rewarder of them that diligently seek him." Here a comma is provided, and the comma can be justified on grammatical grounds since it precedes a conjunction joining two complementary but not identical ideas, namely, the idea that God is (or exists), and the idea that God rewards those who seek the divine Presence. The comma, however, does not help us to see the logical construction of the sentence. It does not help us to make out the movement of thought in the sentence as a whole. And, consequently, it gives us virtually no help in determining how to phrase the sentence when we speak it.

What the sentence plainly asserts is that those who come to God must do two things: First, they must believe that God exists; second, they must believe that those who seek God are rewarded by God. The movement of thought in the sentence is a movement from identification of the subject or actor (the one who comes to God), to a statement about that subject or actor, specifically what she or he must believe. The sentence, therefore, should be phrased in this way (and please note as you read that the solidus through a line of the text indicates where a phrase break occurs): "Whoever would draw near to God / must believe that he exists and that he rewards those who seek him." There could be a very slight pause after "exists" to distinguish between the two things the seeker of God must believe, but, for the reasons just cited, the major phrase break should occur between "God" and "must."

Let us explore what belongs with what in another verse from Scripture, one with which I am sure we are all very familiar: "They went with haste, and found Mary and Joseph, and the babe lying in a manger" (Luke 2:16). Clearly the problem to be avoided in speaking this verse is the crowding of the manger. How do we keep the baby in it and at the same time keep Mary and Joseph out of it? The comma, in this particular instance, is placed helpfully, for the primary phrase break or pause occurs between "Joseph" and "and," where the comma appears. And the words "and the baby lying in a manger'' are said together without any phrase break at all.

Despite the help provided by the comma, however, I have often heard this passage read as follows: "They went with haste/and found Mary and Joseph and the babe lying in a manger." Why is this passage so frequently read as if the baby Jesus' parents were cramped in the manger with the child? May I suggest that a possible cause may be a failure on the part of readers to see the action the words describe? After all, when we read a text, we are not simply speaking words, we are delineating ideas, as was the case with the Hebrews passage, or we are describing actions as is the case here. And when we are describing actions, our first duty is to see with our mind's eye what we are describing so that when we speak, others may see it with us.

Look at the actions depicted in this short verse. Watch them in the theater of your mind. The shepherds rush to Bethlehem. That's the initial bit of action. There, in the place of Jesus' birth, they see Mary, and also Joseph, with Mary, obviously, but not necessarily right next to her. That's the next bit of action. Then, at last, they see the Christ child in the manger, the last bit of action. If you focus sequentially, but not ploddingly, on each piece of action, you will keep each person in the scene where he or she belongs. You will not crowd the manger, you will not blur the scene for your listeners, and you will not talk nonsense.

Perhaps one of the most difficult assignments in phrasing is the handling of detailed, parenthetical expressions. These can be common in texts of Scripture and they can be the bane of the reader's existence. Take for instance this passage: "Elijah took twelve stones, according to the number of the tribes of the sons of Jacob, to whom the word of the Lord came, saying, 'Israel shall be your name'; and with the stones he built an altar in the name of the Lord" (I Kings 18:31-32). It is possible to get so absorbed with the details of the extended parenthetical expression, which begins with the words "according to the number" and which ends with the words "Israel shall be your name," that the movement of thought in the passage as a whole is obscured. Then, too, it is possible to rush through the parenthetical expression and blur details essential to appreciating fully the drama of the passage.

What is to be done? Right away, it needs to be observed that the essential action of the passage is expressed in just two clauses: "Elijah took twelve stones" and "with the stones he built an altar in the name of the Lord." Every other word in the passage is vital for grasping what the action just stated symbolized for Elijah and the people of Israel, but none of those other words actually contributes to evoking the action. Consequently, what the reader needs to do is start the action, saying, "Elijah took twelve stones." Then, however, the reader immediately needs to stop the action, leave it incomplete, suspended, like a "freeze frame" on television or in the movies, while carefully yet spiritedly giving the information concerning what the selection of the twelve stones signified to Elijah and the rest of the people gathered on Mount Carmel. Finally the reader needs to resume the action almost as if the fill-in information had not been given, speaking in the same tone of voice and with the same rate of delivery he or she used in giving the opening line. A visualization of such a reading of I Kings 18:31-32 might look like this:

ELIJAH TOOK TWELVE STONES

according to the number of the tribes of the sons of Jacob, to whom the word of the Lord came, saying, "Israel shall be your name";

AND WITH THE STONES HE BUILT AN ALTAR IN THE NAME OF THE LORD.

So far, in discussing what belongs with what when we speak written texts, we have looked at the movement of ideas and the development of dramatic action in passages, and we have talked about what to do with long, detailed parenthetical expressions. The next problem we will delve into has to do with connecting words. What do we do with them? Here, for example, is a statement by the apostle Paul containing the connecting word *that*. "I find it to be a law that when I want to do right, evil lies close at hand" (Rom. 7:21). Sometimes you will find people who pause both before and after the connecting word. Thus, in the case of the quotation we are considering from Romans, they would turn the word "that" into a one-word phrase. Such a practice may not make utter nonsense of the sentence, but it certainly sounds very pedantic.

In fact, though some do read that way, nobody really talks that way. And in reading aloud, the object is to come as close as possible to sounding conversational. There are occasions in conversation when a connecting word is put with the phrase that precedes it. So one might say, using Paul's words, "I find it to be a law that/when I want to do right, evil lies close at hand." However, no one phrases statements that way in conversation unless she or he does not know how the thought is going to be completed. The pause after the connecting word actually happens because the person doing the pausing has not yet figured out what to say next. Furthermore, when a usually inadvertent and awkward pause after a connecting word such as "that" occurs, you will notice that the speaker, as a rule, leaves his or her pitch up, suspending the "that" in mid air. The suspension of the "that" serves to indicate that the "that" really needs to be connected with what is coming. The person might even repeat the "that" several times until a way to finish the sentence has been found.

If Paul's statement were an instance of hesitant, extemporaneous speech, you might hear something like this: "I find it to be a law that . . . that . . . well, that . . . that when I want to do right, evil is close at hand." Clearly, the connecting word actually belongs with the phrase that follows it. It is the means by which that phrase gets added to what has already been said. The most meaningful and conversational way to phrase the sentence from Romans we have been dealing with, therefore, is as follows: "I find it to be a law/that when I want to do right/evil lies close at hand."

A more common error than pausing after a connecting word like *that*, however, is the habit of pausing after the word introducing a quotation. In order to explore this problem, look for a moment at the following verses from Matthew's account of the gospel. "He opened his mouth and taught them, saying: 'Blessed are the poor in spirit,'" (Matt. 5:2-3). Time after time you may hear verses such as these spoken with the following phrasing: "He opened his mouth and taught them saying/'Blessed are the poor in spirit.' " Additionally, the error is often compounded by the use of a downward inflection on the word *saying.* Thus we end up with an opening phrase that simply does not make sense: "He opened his mouth and taught them saying."

Plainly, he did not open his mouth and teach them "not saying." That is, he did not teach by keeping silent, by just standing there with his mouth open! Of course he was "saying," but the point is, he was saying *something.* The "saying" goes with what was said. It does not go with the preceding words of the sentence. The best way to keep the connecting word *saying* attached to what comes after it, I think, is to treat it as a verbal quotation mark. As we all know, a quotation mark goes with the quotation it identifies. It does not go with the lines leading up to the quotation. A more intelligible phrasing of the two verses from Matthew we have been discussing consequently would go like this: "He opened his mouth and taught them/saying: 'Blessed are the poor in spirit.' "

Because the verbal quotation mark is so frequently handled clumsily, let me provide one more illustration of its more adroit use. Here is a brief passage from Luke's account of the gospel: "Now the tax collectors and sinners were all drawing near to hear him. And the Pharisees and the scribes murmured, saying, 'This man receives sinners and eats with them' " (Luke 15:1-2). In this case, the punctuation of the sentence provides half a clue for us, for there is a comma after "murmured" and before "saying" where the reader's phrase break should occur. But you would not pause at the comma following the word *saying.* Instead, to sound conversational and not stilted, and because a verbal quotation mark belongs with the quotation itself, you would attach *saying* to the statement that follows it. The sentence thus would be phrased: "And the Pharisees and the scribes murmured/saying 'This man receives sinners and eats with them.' "

In discussing phrasing, we have stressed the need to group

words into easily understood units of thought that tell one thing at a time. That is, we have to determine what belongs with what. In order to determine what belongs with what, I suggested that we attempt to get inside the development of thought or action in a passage so that, in speaking the written word, we can delineate that thought or evoke that action for others. Our speech, after all, is not simply a stringing together of words. It is a manifestation of our understanding. We depict with the spoken word what we see with our mind's eye. Two particular problems in phrasing were then explored, the problem of the long, detailed parenthetical expression and the problem of the connecting word. We saw that the connecting word typically goes with the phrase that follows it, while the parenthetical expression gets set off from the basic flow of thought or action in a passage when the speaker abruptly halts that flow, gives the details of the parenthesis, and then returns to the basic flow of thought or action almost as if the parenthetical information had not been given. In order to accomplish all that, however, the speaker needs to have sufficient breath control. And that is what I would like to talk about as the final topic of this chapter. Simply put, breathing must be related to phrasing.

We have all heard beginning singers taking breaths in odd places; in the middle of phrases, for example, instead of between them—sometimes even in the middle of words. We may forgive them if their voices are sufficiently beautiful. We may, as they sing, willingly do their thinking for them. Listeners may do readers' thinking for them too, patching together broken phrases and figuring out what was meant despite what was said. That is a wearisome task, however, and listeners cannot be expected to stay with it very long.

To save listeners that trouble, readers need to anticipate where they are going in expressing a thought. The end of the thought needs to be in view from the beginning, and concentration needs to be sustained right up to and, indeed, into the pause after the phrase has been spoken. Sometimes, for the sake of progression of thought and dramatic action, several phrases may be linked, a pause coming only at the completion of the whole series of linked phrases. Here again, if, as the series of phrases is begun, the reader keeps in mind where that series will end, there is greater likelihood that she or he will have sufficient breath to manage it all without anxiety or hurry.

It must be kept in mind that in speaking the written word, every phrase is related to every other phrase. Readers must understand that relationship and bend every effort to make sure that pauses for breath do not interfere with it. I have chosen a passage from the conclusion of Jesus' Sermon on the Mount to illustrate the relationship between adequate breath control and the linking of phrases in order to facilitate progression of thought. The passage reads as follows:

Every one . . . who hears these words of mine and does them will be like a wise man who built his house upon the rock; and the rain fell, and the floods came, and the winds blew and beat upon that house, but it did not fall, because it had been founded on the rock. And everyone who hears these words of mine and does not do them will be like a foolish man who built his house upon the sand; and the rain fell, and the floods came, and the winds blew and beat against that house, and it fell; and great was the fall of it. (Matt. 7:24-27)

It is obvious to us all, I think, that this text of Scripture features parallel construction of thought. The first half of the passage illustrates how a person who hears and does Jesus' words, like a wise individual who builds a house on a solid foundation, can withstand severe mistreatment by powerful forces and yet endure. The second half of the passage shows how failing to hear and do Jesus' word can end in ruin, just as the house of a foolish individual, built on a faulty foundation, collapses when rains and floods come and when fierce winds blow and beat against it.

The thing the two halves of this teaching of Jesus have in common is the storm, and it ought to sound like a storm, it ought move like a storm when it is spoken. The falling rains, the rising floods, and the driving winds are not separate items on a laundry list, they are integral parts of one potentially devastating natural disaster. They occur all at once. And there needs to be a building up of suspense until we see what happens to the house built on a firm foundation (almost surprisingly it stands) and to the house built on sand(it falls, catastrophically). To keep the storm raging up to the point of climax—the surprising endurance of the first house, the catastrophic ruin of the second—it is important not to pause at every possible pausing place, not to stop for a breath until the climactic point is reached. Therefore, one would not say, for example, "And the rain fell/and the floods came/ and the winds blew/and beat upon that house/but it did not fall." Rather one would say, "And the rain fell and the floods came and the winds blew and beat upon that house/ but it did not fall." In a word, the storm would need to rage in one intense, moving, yet not rushed phrase, supported by one continuous flow of breath.

To wrap up this chapter on phrasing and the relationship of breathing to phrasing, I have laid out, with suggested phrase breaks, the passage from Matthew's Gospel dealing with those who hear and do Jesus' word and those who hear and do not do it. A single solidus through a line of text continues to indicate where a pause should occur. A double solidus indicates a slightly longer, more dramatic pause at a point of major transition in the development of thought. A dotted solidus indicates where a phrase break may or may not be placed according to the discretion of the reader. No doubt other approaches to phrasing this passage than the one I am offering could be found, but the one offered here is in keeping with the principles discussed in this chapter and may serve as a useful model for those wishing to rethink their habits of phrasing and perhaps to modify them in the interest of being clearer when they speak the written word.

> Every one . . . who hears these words of mine ⫶ and does them / will be like a wise man ⫶ who built his house upon the rock; // and the rain fell and the floods came and the winds blew and beat upon that house // but it did not fall / because it had been founded on the rock. // And every one who hears these words of mine ⫶ and does not do them / will be like a foolish man ⫶ who built his house upon the sand; // and the rain fell and the floods came and the winds blew and beat against that house // and it fell / and great was the fall of it.

CHAPTER FOUR

BASIC CONSIDERATIONS IN SPEAKING THE WRITTEN WORD: EMPHASIS

You will recall from the discussion in the preceding chapter that phrasing arranges words into easily understood units of thought that tell one thing at a time. Emphasis determines what word within a phrase receives primary consideration. When a word is emphasized, it is lifted into prominence and arrests attention. Emphasis thus is used to discriminate the most important idea from all related ideas. Of course, it is also possible to identify secondary, even tertiary emphases and de-emphasized, unstressed syllables, thereby determining the meter or cadence of the spoken word. We are not going into such fine discriminations here, however, for our concern is not with detailed phonetic analysis (the study of the sound structure of discourse), but with the perception and expression of meaning. We are concerned with finding out how to focus attention on what our listeners need to attend to when we speak so that they may follow our line of thought.

We all have developed ways of doing that in everyday conversation. Without thinking about it very much at all, we manage to speak so that people understand us and respond to us appropriately. For instance, when, at the dinner table, we say, "Please pass the salt," automatically we emphasize the word *salt*, and we get what we want. We would not say, "Please pass *the* salt," as if there were some other or lesser salt that could be passed to us; nor would we say, "please *pass* the salt," as if the salt could get to us by some means other than by being passed. No, in conversation, we know what we mean and as a rule we say what we mean.

Furthermore, we manage to change subtly the way we emphasize words so that not only is our meaning clear, but also our attitude toward our listeners. At our own family dinner table, where we are familiar with one another and where informality is expected, we say, "Please pass the *salt*," and emphasize the word *salt* by increasing volume slightly on that word and by using a downward inflection. The tone is one of gentle, matter-of-fact assertion or command. But if we are at a formal dinner where almost everyone is a stranger, we may say, "Please pass the *salt*," with an upward inflection, a rising pitch on the word *salt*, thereby showing deference. The tone is nearly that of a question instead of assertion, a request instead of a command. So, in conversation, habitually we say what we mean and we do so in a manner fit for the occasion.

On the other hand, when we are speaking other people's thoughts, when we are reading texts in large part prepared by persons other than ourselves, as generally is the case in worship, we cannot assume that our conversational habits will stick with us. Instead, our reading habits, as a rule, take over, and what we emphasize and how we emphasize it may seem stilted, nonconversational, even inaccurate and bewildering. For instance, I have heard this passage read and emphasized this way: "Peace I leave *with* you; my peace I give *to* you; not as the world gives do I give to *you*" (John 14:27). Later I will try to demonstrate what might be a more helpful way to handle emphasis in this passage so that the development of thought is clear instead of obscure. For the present though, let us simply observe that the emphasis, placed as it is on two prepositions and a pronoun, muddles the thought for the listener. Could that be so because the thought is already a muddle for the speaker?

It is possible to read words thoughtlessly. "Words, words, words!" a minister friend of mine recently complained. "Protestant worship especially seems to be nothing but words, too many words and not enough ideas, feelings, deeds." The minister may have a point, yet one obviously cannot do without words in worship any more than one can do without notes in music. One does not say of a composition by Mozart, "too many notes," unless, of course, one wishes to appear foolish. So also one does not say of the Apostles' Creed "too many words." For the issue is not one of quantity, but of quality. How are the words used? That's the question. How are they spoken? What words receive emphasis, why, and how?

As I have said, in conversation, for most of us most of the time, it is all quite automatic. But in reading, too often, words are spoken as if the thoughts inspiring them have not actually been thought, felt, responded to by the speaker. The speaker simply locks into "reading gear," and from then on it is "off to the races" and let the listener catch whatever she or he can as the words and ideas fly by. To correct that problem, we need to give conscious attention to what in conversation seems so automatic. We need to explore the means of emphasis and their appropriate use with a variety of texts. As we do so, bear in mind that our discussion, for the sake of simplicity and clarity, necessarily will involve categorizing and describing the means of emphasis in a somewhat artificial way. In actual speech, the means of emphasis are not experienced independently from one another. Instead they are experienced together and their effects are felt simultaneously.

The means of emphasis are stress (typically increase of intensity and volume on a word), pause (usually coupled with a lengthening or stretching of vowel sound on the word being emphasized), and inflection (pitch change on a single word or syllable). Stress as a means of emphasis characteristically gives vitality, physical energy, assertive, even aggressive purpose to a word or thought. The degree of increase in volume may or may not be great, depending on the context within which the word being spoken is emphasized. But the increase in intensity, whether with great or moderate volume, as a rule, needs to be discernible. For example, the following brief excerpt from I Samuel would not actually have to be yelled for the thought to be expressed clearly, but the speaker would need to have plenty of intensity throughout and especially on the emphasized (italicized) words: "*Goliath* . . . *stood* and *shouted* to the *ranks* of *Israel*, '*Why* have you come out to draw up for *battle?*' " (17:4, 8).

How is increase in intensity obtained? It is obtained by a fierce concentration on the thought and one's purpose in speaking it (in this case, to intimidate Israel), and by increase in physical energy in breath control (as singers say, "tighten the gut"), articulation, body posture, and facial expression. One cannot use a breathy voice and a slack jaw, rock back on one's heels, draw a blank on one's face, and speak Goliath's words in any way commensurate with their intended effect. Goliath intends to strike terror in the hearts of Israel's warriors, and people listening to the story as it is read or told need to be made aware of that. In classical, rhetorical terms, stress is an emotional means of emphasis. It signifies movement, a change in one's being, even in one's physical condition.

In saying that, I know that there are some who are exceedingly wary of "appeals to the emotions," any tapping of people's capacity to be changed. The problem, however, is not with emotion, movement, or change *per se*, but with inappropriate emotion, that is, movement or change not grounded in and justified by the plain sense and significance of what is being said. Additionally, it should be noted that inappropriate emotion, movement, or change can be as much a matter of understatement as overstatement. In other words, to read Goliath's lines as if they were meant to put Israel to sleep or to instruct Israel in a dispassionate way concerning her military options would be to misread them entirely. The effect of such a reading, in fact, would quite obviously be ludicrous.

To read Goliath's words right, stress as a means of emphasis would have to be employed, but it would have to be employed accurately to make the sense of the passage clear. It would also have to be employed in a manner suited to one's physical and liturgical setting. For example, volume would probably not be increased greatly in a sanctuary sixty feet square, with a dozen or so worshipers present, all of whom had just finished singing a meditative hymn. In such a case, some increase in intensity alone definitely would suffice to stress the appropriate words and ideas in Goliath's statement. To harken back to what was said in chapter 2, the worship leader speaking Goliath's lines would have to be responsive both to the interpretative demands of the passage and the situational constraints of the service of worship. Furthermore, as I have said before, there are no easy, safe, universally applicable rules for exercising that responsibility. To the contrary, to lead in the service of worship is precisely to exercise that responsibility freely.

The second means of emphasis is the pause. If stress is an

emotional, vital means of emphasis, particularly meant to evoke change in others, then, in traditional rhetorical terms, pause is an "ethical" or "moral" means of emphasis—not so much in the strict, literal sense of ethics and morality as in the more general sense of valuing, savoring, holding dear. When someone pauses before or after a thought, the listener immediately intuits that the thought is of considerable value to the speaker. It appears to be a matter of substantial personal consequence. The thought itself may be happy or sad, beautiful or ugly, humane or pernicious, and the speaker may detest it or rejoice in it. Be that as it may, its weight in the body of all the speaker is saying is considerable. Also, indirectly, it may disclose the speaker's ethical stance, his or her attitude toward life and other people, toward God.

Surely, when Job says, "Why did I not die at birth, come forth from the womb and expire?" (Job 3:11), one gets a pretty clear idea of what the man thinks about his life—and about God! The pauses after "birth" and before "and expire," if one were to use such, certainly would be value-laden, dramatic, indicative of what was of great moment to this most famous sufferer. Or when the psalmist says, "The Lord is my shepherd, I shall not want" (Ps. 23:1), and the person speaking the psalmist's words pauses after "shepherd" and "want," the listener, no doubt, is made aware that the psalmist appreciates God's shepherding and that the psalmist holds dear the promise of deliverance from deprivation.

The same holds true for us all, I believe. When an idea has great significance for us, we pause before it or after it. We hang on to the idea, which is why pauses are so often coupled with a lengthening or stretching of vowel sound in the word or words being emphasized through use of the pause. We take the thought to heart. Perhaps we are even reluctant to let it go, to express it at all. Notice how much pause there is in the utterance of someone stricken with grief, or awed by the almost ineffable beauty of dark, bare branches against a winter sky. Of course I am speaking here of pauses that are meant, intended. I am speaking of pauses that are in fact clues to meaning, to the sense and significance of words. I am not referring here to inadvertent pauses, dead spots, "black holes" for words.

A pause should be alive. It should be a meaningful silence. Before an idea, a pause prepares the hearer. It builds expectancy. After an idea, it provides an opportunity for the thought to germinate. Furthermore, in the pause, something happens to the speaker. This is no time for empty-eyed staring into space. This is a time for assimilating the object of consideration. This is a time for responding to that assimilated object and for manifesting one's response in face and body. W. J. Beeners, Professor of Speech at Princeton Theological Seminary, has said that the secret of poise is pause. With a pause a speaker takes time to get and hold a thought before expressing it, while listeners take time to assess what has already been expressed and to get ready for whatever is coming next.

The third and last means of emphasis is inflection. As I am using the term, *inflection* refers to the movement of pitch higher or lower on a single word or syllable in order to make clear the development of thought in a passage. The movement of pitch over a whole phrase or series of phrases, I prefer to call intonational pattern or speech melody.

Intonational patterns are better treated in a more technical manual on phonetic analysis and transcription of the spoken word. Our distinctions are less refined. We are concerned with pitch change, which clearly takes a word out of the intonational pattern or melody line established by the speaker and thus causes that word, as it were, to stand at attention while the rest of the words in the phrase march on.

Pitch, you will discover, is a dominating means of emphasis. Stress and pause may be used with it to lift a word into prominence, but neither stress nor pause alone can suffice to give emphasis to a word if, on some other word, there is a radical movement of pitch. Instead, that word spoken with the radical movement of pitch will stand out. The following exercise illustrates what I mean. Speak this sentence six times in succession: John is driving down town today. The first time you say the sentence, put the emphasis on *John*. The second time you say it, put the emphasis on *is*. The third time you say it, put the emphasis on *driving*. Continue speaking the sentence until each word in it has been emphasized in turn. I am sure you will find that you cannot shift the emphasis to each word in turn unless you raise the pitch on the word you wish to emphasize. If you shout the word *John* for instance, but raise pitch on the word *town, town* will be lifted into prominence and will arrest attention. Or if you pause before *is* and shout the word *is* besides, but again raise pitch on the word *town, town* once more will receive emphasis, not *is*.

You may even discover that you are having trouble varying the pitch on the word you wish to emphasize, whichever it is. If you are having such trouble, the reason may be that the seemingly "natural" or, more accurately, "habitual" way of speaking a sentence such as "John is driving down town today," is with emphasis on the word *town*, the last word in the basic unit of thought. *Today*, the last word in the sentence, nearly seems to be an addendum to the basic thought. The sentence tells us what John is doing. He is driving down town. The addendum tells us when he is doing it, merely clarifying the present tense of the verb *is*.

However, if you think of the statement "John is driving down town today" not as an assertion with no reason for being, but as a reply to a question or statement made by someone else, the possibility of willfully changing pitch appropriately on each successive word as the sentence is spoken six times, is increased. To illustrate, if someone says to you, "*Who* is driving down town today?" and you reply, "*John* is driving down town today," your pitch probably rises on the word *John*. Similarly, if someone says to you, "John is *not* driving down town today," and you argue back, "John *is* driving down town today," your pitch in all likelihood will rise on the word *is*. In a word, emphasis is determined by considering a broad setting, not just the phrase or even the sentence itself.

Pitch is always the dominating means of emphasis. Stress and pause may color emphasis, give it vitality or weight, "emotional" or "ethical" connotation, but it is inflection, the movement of pitch on a single word or syllable, that truly highlights the development of thought in a passage, riveting our attention to the words that bring out the sense of a text. To return once again to traditional rhetorical terms, inflection is a logical or intellectual means of emphasis. Used right, it directs a listener's attention to what a passage actually says and so helps to keep emotional and ethical (or valuative) connotation in check, ostensibly grounded in intellectual content.

There are three primary types of inflection—rising, falling, and circumflex (the movement of pitch both downward and upward on a single word or syllable). Rising inflections ask questions, defer to the will of the hearer, or leave thoughts incomplete, tentative. Falling inflections make assertions, declare the will of the speaker, and complete thoughts. Circumflex inflections suggest complexity of thought. The "hmm" you mumble when you are trying to figure out for yourself what a person "really meant in saying that" is an instance of circumflex inflection.

Once again, in conversation, almost automatically we use inflections purposefully and appropriately. They just seem to come out right. Strangely, however, in reading aloud we can get into trouble using stereotyped and predictable inflections. Our oral reading consequently may sound too much like reading and not sufficiently like talking sense. Thoughts may fail to have that alive, first-time, just-discovered character about them. Even more crucially, they may not seem logically related to one another. In other words, the oral reader may appear not to be thinking as she or he reads.

Or worse, instead of being delivered in a straightforward manner, thoughts (or rather sounds) could seem to be "intoned." That is, inflectional patterns could be varied but not according to sense. How discouraging it is that the last problem is typically labeled "preachery tone." What we need, of course, is inflection appropriate to the sense of what we are speaking. We do not need fixed, habitual patterns of inflection superimposed on our material.

To get a feel for how devastating fixed inflectional patterns can be, try reading aloud the following traditional collect or short prayer three times, each time putting emphasis on the last word of each phrase and using only one type of inflection all the way through. The first time through, use an upward inflection on the last word of each phrase. I will mark this inflection with an arrow (◡). The second time through, use all downward inflections (⌒). The third time through, use circumflex inflections (⌒⌣).

Speaking a collect with upward inflections on the last word of all phrases:

Almighty God (⌣) unto whom all hearts are open (⌣)
all desires known (⌣) and from whom no secrets
are hid (⌣): Cleanse the thoughts of our hearts (⌣)
by the inspiration of your Holy Spirit (⌣)
that we may perfectly love you (⌣) and worthily
magnify your holy name (⌣)
through Jesus Christ our Lord (⌣). Amen (⌣).

Speaking a collect with downward inflections on the last word of all phrases:

Almighty God (⌒) unto whom all hearts are open (⌒)
all desires known (⌒) and from whom no secrets
are hid (⌒): Cleanse the thoughts of our
hearts (⌒) by the inspiration of your Holy
Spirit (⌒) that we may perfectly love you (⌒)
and worthily magnify your holy name (⌒)
through Jesus Christ our Lord (⌒). Amen (⌒).

Speaking a collect with circumflex inflections on the last word of all phrases:

Almighty God (⌒⌣) unto whom all hearts are
open (⌒⌣) all desires known (⌒⌣) and from
whom no secrets are hid (⌒⌣): Cleanse the
thoughts of our hearts (⌒⌣) by the inspiration
of your Holy Spirit (⌒⌣) that we may perfectly
love you (⌒⌣) and worthily magnify your holy
name (⌒⌣) through Jesus Christ our Lord (⌒⌣).
Amen (⌒⌣).

It would not surprise me if you found this exercise, which makes use of a beautiful and profound prayer, coming near to sacrilege. Yet, in truth, this prayer and others like it all too often are read aloud in worship in a manner very close to the manner in which I have instructed you. The first reading makes everything sound like a surprise or, at best, a tentative, insecure statement. The second makes everything sound just the opposite, determined, rigid, fixed, secure, deadly. The third, dare I say it, at times seems to imply that the divine has a nearly prurient interest in the details and complexities of our secret lives. Such distortions can occur when inflection follows stereotyped reading patterns or when it is used in an attempt to establish attitude or mood instead of to direct the listener's mind to the contemplation of thoughts and their relationships to one another. Keep in mind, then, that inflection (pitch change on a single word or syllable) is for the most part a logical or intellectual means of emphasis, and that stress and pause need to be used with it when one desires to give emotional or valuative coloring to the communication of ideas through the spoken word.

So far we have discussed the means of emphasis: stress, pause, and inflection. Now, to conclude this chapter on emphasis, we must explore how those means are to be employed. In other words, how do we determine where to place primary emphasis when we are speaking the written word? To answer that question, I would like to return to the sentence from the Gospel of John which, at the very beginning of this chapter, was inappropriately emphasized as follows: "Peace I leave *with* you; my peace I give *to* you; not as the world gives do I give to *you*" (John 14:27). You will recall that the emphases on the prepositions *with* and *to* and the final emphasis on the pronoun *you* did not make sense but obscured it. Why? Why did those emphases fail to make sense? Why were they—and are they—inappropriate?

The reason, I suggest, is threefold: (1) The emphases do not make clear what is being talked about. They do not identify the subject of the sentence. (I am using the word *subject* here not merely grammatically, but substantively, to refer to the thematic content of the sentence.) (2) The emphases do not make clear whether there are any modifications (expansions of thought, contractions of thought, comparisons or contrasts of thought) in the subject being discussed. (3) The emphases do not make clear the essential qualities of the action, if any, which are or ought to be undertaken in relation to the subject. The emphases do not make sense because they do not reveal the oral reader's involvement with the substance of the sentence, the development of thought in the sentence. They only reveal that the oral reader knows how to say the words of the sentence. Put another way, the reading is superficial.

To get past superficiality, to get past a mere statement of words to a statement of the thought the words are meant to express, what one has to do is make clear precisely those things not made clear in the original reading. One has to determine what is being talked about, the subject. One has to determine what modifications, if any, are given regarding that subject. And one has to determine the essential qualities of the action (if there are any), which are or ought to be undertaken in relation to the subject.

· Surely the subject of this sentence from John's Gospel is peace. In the first phrase spoken, then, *peace* would be the word to emphasize. Pitch would be raised on the word *peace*, and there might be a short pause after the word disclosing the value of the word (or, more accurately, the thought or subject) for the speaker. We can show how to say it this way: "*Peace* I leave with you." Next, in the second phrase, we get a modification of the subject. Jesus is not just talking about peace. He is talking about his own peace, "My peace," as he puts it. The second phrase thus should be rendered, "*My* peace I give to you." Then how is this peace given? What is the quality of the action undertaken in relation to the subject at hand? The answer is expressed in negative terms. Jesus says that his peace is given differently from the way the world gives peace. So the word *world* should receive primary emphasis in the last phrase as follows: "Not as the *world* gives do I give to you." And remember, to emphasize the word *world*, you will need to raise the pitch on it (probably a circumflex inflection would be best) so that it stands up out of the intonational pattern of the phrase as a whole. To put it all together, this brief passage from John's Gospel would be read with emphasis on the words as marked here: "*Peace* I leave with you; *my* peace I give to you; not as the *world* gives do I give to you."

An interesting twist on the relationship of a subject to the action undertaken relative to that subject is provided by a brief excerpt from the account of the contest between Elijah and the prophets of Baal on Mount Carmel. At one point in the contest, Elijah turns on the people of Israel and says, "If the Lord is God, follow him; but if Baal, then follow him" (I Kings 18:21). I have heard the passage handled with emphasis on these words in sequence: *Lord, him, Baal, him.* Such a pattern of emphasis makes sense up to a point, for it does bring out that either Yahweh or Baal is truly God and should be followed. But it also misses something very essential, namely the quality of action, of challenge and response, which plainly runs through the passage depicting the struggle on Mount Carmel. In other words, it removes the choice of the people of Israel from the existential level, the level of life and death, and places it in the realm of the intellect alone.

Yahweh and Baal are offered as equal options and one is left to choose the religious option which best pleases him or her. But on Mount Carmel, the people are not in a position to choose dispassionately between equally valid options. No, on Mount Carmel, and in your life and mine too, either Yahweh (the Lord) is God and should be *followed,* or Baal is god and *he* should be followed. That is, if you choose God, you have to *follow* God. That is the consequence of your choice. In life and in death you either are or are not God's. To keep action and consequence at the fore, to keep the issue before the people on Mount Carmel one of gut reaction instead of mere intellectual contemplation, therefore, the placement of emphasis in the passage needs to be handled in this manner: "If the Lord is God, *follow* him; but if Baal, then follow *him.*"

Emphasis, even given the three principles of determining subject, modifier of subject, and action relative to subject, cannot be worked out without considering what is demanded of us in the broader literary context. To read any part of a text, that is to say, whether the text be a passage of Scripture, a call to worship, or a prayer or benediction, one needs to have an understanding of the text in its entirety. Generally, in each successive phrase, one emphasizes those words that bring out what is new, that heighten comparisons or contrasts or modifications of thought, or that in some way indicate challenge and response, cause and effect. But all this is done with an appreciation for how each phrase, each sentence, each paragraph contributes to the development of thought (that is, the progression of ideas, feelings, and actions), in the passage as a whole.

As I have tried to show, the means of emphasis—stress, pause, and inflection—cover the gamut of human motivations. To use them responsibly is necessarily to be involved fully in the emotional, valuative (or ethical), and intellectual content of the text one is trying to read. This is why we cannot reduce principles to rules or suggest that there is a way to handle either phrasing or emphasis, which, once understood, will not require of any of us the always strenuous and fresh investment of body, heart, and mind in the task of discerning and expressing the movement of thought in passages. For that is precisely what is required.

In the remaining chapters of this book, we will discuss calls to worship, benedictions, prayers, Scripture readings, and the celebration of the sacraments of baptism and communion. What is vital in all of it is all of *us*, the whole of us, every aspect of our being. From the task of effective speech communication in leading worship, the "you" of you and me can never be withdrawn.

CHAPTER FIVE

SPEAKING CALLS TO WORSHIP AND BENEDICTIONS

A t the start of his novel *In the Beginning*, Chaim Potok makes the assertion, "All beginnings are hard." Well, in worship, beginnings may not be hard, but they are not exactly easy either. That is to say, one cannot take lightly the assignment of handling a call to worship. It is not a grim, arduous task certainly, but it is a significant task, for it sets the tone, the mood, the expectation of the congregation for all that is to follow. The call to worship is not quite so simple as saying "Hello" or "Hi" to someone any more than the benediction at the close of worship is like saying "so long." We do not begin worship with a folksy "Good to see ya!" and we do not end it with "Have a nice day!" Instead, as worship begins, the focus of attention is on God, who God is, and who we are as a people gathered in the divine name. And worship ends with the blessing of God's presence promised and secured to every single worshiper and to the gathered community as a whole.

What could be more momentous for persons met to worship God than to hear words such as these: "As one whom his mother comforts, so I will comfort you; [and] you shall be comforted" (Isa. 66:13)? Or to hear, as the service of worship concludes: "Grace, mercy and peace from God the Father, God the Son and God the Holy Spirit be with you all"?

Beginnings and endings in worship are of a piece, for worship has its alpha and its omega in the One who occasions it. Nowhere is the divine initiative and human response more clearly evident than in the speaking of calls to worship and benedictions, for it is God who gathers us to hear the Word by which we are constituted as a community of faith. And it is God who scatters us abroad, not as isolated individuals who must do our best to please our Sovereign, but as persons in relationship who can expect to encounter the divine Presence again and again in the caring and the cares of those around us, our neighbors. The call to worship is a call to worship *God*, and the benediction is the solemn blessing of God. It is the bracing affirmation of "God with us" always, in judgment and mercy, in challenge and succor. The response of the congregation in word or song, silence or action, therefore, is a resounding "Amen!" So be it!

The call to worship and the benediction are spoken to the congregation as a congregation, as a worshiping and serving community. They are not spoken simply to a collection of individual friends and acquaintances. Consequently, though there ought to be some measure of cordiality and welcome evidenced in the call and some measure of friendship and good will evidenced in the benediction, there needs to be much more as well. There needs to be an awareness of family, not of family in the strictly social and customary sense, but of family in the theological sense. The people gathered for worship, whatever their differences, however much they may like or dislike one another, approve or disapprove of one another, are the familial fellowship of the kingdom of God. Jesus expressed it this way: "Whoever does the will of God is my brother, and sister, and mother" (Mark 3:35). To look at a congregation gathered for worship as young and old, rich and poor, affable and austere siblings in Christ is to look at a congregation in terms of its uniquely Christian identity and purpose. And to speak a call to worship or a benediction to such a gathering is to remind that gathering of what it is and what it has been called, set apart, made holy to do.

That is an awesome responsibility. It is a responsibility that lifts the speaker above his or her personal sentiments and feelings toward individuals in the church. It is a responsibility that centers the speaker in Christ. After all, it is in Christ that the divine word has been spoken, which has made the people of the church God's own. It is in Christ that the people of the church have been given their identity, however much they may fail to measure up to it. It is in Christ that they have been charged with their responsibility to exercise the reign of God among the people of the earth. And, even when only two or three of them are met in Christ's name, Christ has promised nevertheless to be present in their midst. I shall put it starkly. To welcome a congregation to worship is to speak in the name of Christ and on Christ's behalf. And to speak the benediction to a worshiping congregation is to bless people in Christ's name and to acknowledge publicly this greatest mystery of faith, that the dwelling of God is with human beings.

From this it ought to be clear that, in speaking calls to worship and benedictions, what one says and how one says it are not matters of personal preference and taste merely. They are matters of theological and ecclesial import. Indeed, the speaking of calls to worship and benedictions is the doing of theology. Furthermore, whether the person doing that theology is a member of the laity or the clergy, he or she is a servant or minister of the church and is accountable to the church. He or she is a servant of Christ and is accountable to Christ.

In speaking calls to worship and benedictions, then, the first thing we need to do is to determine what to say. Fortunately the church has not left us at a loss here. Rather it has provided us with rich denominational and ecumenical helps, chiefly our Scriptures, of course, but also our hymnbooks and service books and various seasonal resources for the Christian year. Some ecclesiastical traditions specify what should be said as a call to worship or benediction on a given Lord's day or other occasion of worship. Whether one belongs to such a tradition or not, however, it would seem wise to avail oneself of the guides and helps the church provides. For one thing, those guides and helps are probably a good deal less peculiar and limiting than the imagination and insight of any one person. After all, the church's guides and helps customarily draw on the experience of women and men in the church through the ages.

Additionally, traditional calls to worship and benedictions bind us who speak them to the wider community of faith, which has nurtured us in the things of God and which, through the voice of particular, local congregations, has called us and equipped us to lead in worship. When we speak calls to worship and benedictions, we clearly speak as ourselves, but we do not speak *for* ourselves. Instead, we speak for Christ and the church.

Still, the content of our calls to worship and benedictions cannot be determined exclusively by reliance on received texts. This is because received texts, including passages of Scripture, may not be worded in a way appropriate to these particular liturgical uses. As a result, some editing may be required. For example, on Pentecost Sunday, a worship leader may wish to use as a call to worship the following verse from the prophecy of Joel: "And it shall come to pass afterward, that I will pour out my spirit on all flesh; your sons and your daughters shall prophesy, your old men shall dream dreams, and your young men shall see visions" (2:28).

The first "and" and the "afterward" in the verse link the verse to its context, the specific acts of God's judgment about which the prophet speaks. They do not make sense in the immediate liturgical setting of the call to worship, however. They raise questions that are not going to be answered. The "and" obviously implies a connection of what is said to something preceding the "and." We don't know what that is, and, in the setting of a call to worship, we are not going to find out. The "afterward" immediately raises the question, After *what?* Thus it seems appropriate to leave out the "and" and the "afterward." It also seems appropriate to add a phrase or two to link the scriptural quotation explicitly to its liturgical purpose. So after quoting the verse from Joel, one may say, "Thus says the Lord, and so we worship the Lord our God."

For present-day theological and cultural reasons also, one might wish to edit passages being used as calls to worship or benedictions. I am thinking here specifically of the issue of sex-inclusive language. That is not the only theological matter that ought to be considered in selecting and determining how to use a text of Scripture or any other text as a call to worship or benediction. Other considerations are also important and have already been alluded to. They are the appropriateness of the passage to the liturgical season or theme, the issue of divine initiative and human response, and sensitivity to historical precedent, denominational practice, and ecumenical consensus.

Yet, in our day and cultural setting, no theological issues I can think of have greater import for the way we go about worshiping God than the language we use to talk to God and to one another. Humanly speaking, the congregation to which we speak a call to worship or a benediction is made up of men *and* women, usually more women than men. Theologically speaking, the Christ who is in the midst of the two or three or more gathered for worship is in the midst of them *all*. The Christ may be seen in each of them, for each of them is in Christ. The use of sex-inclusive language in worship, therefore, is not just a matter of tact or politics or even personal conviction. It is a matter of theological and ecclesial integrity. Part of being responsible and accountable as one who leads in worship is to attempt to use language that includes all and not just one-half of humanity.

I mention this in connection with calls to worship and benedictions particularly because calls to worship set the mood and expectation for our services of worship and benedictions send us out from those services blessed, as only God can bless us, with the divine Presence itself. Throughout the service as a whole it is possible, quite imperceptibly, to vary language usage, attempting to maintain a balance between pronouns such as "her" and "him," and nouns such as "man" and "woman," "son" and "daughter," "brother" and "sister," "father" and "mother." Furthermore it is possible to do this both in reference to persons individually and in reference to persons in relationship to one another and to God. But in calls to worship and benedictions, in the beginnings and ends of our services of worship, striving for inclusiveness of expression seems especially warranted.

With benedictions the issue very nearly resolves itself. In the grammar of benedictions, as a rule, use is made of the second person to refer to those being blessed. Typically we say something such as, "The grace of the Lord Jesus Christ and the love of God and the fellowship of the Holy Spirit be with *you* all" (II Cor. 13:14, emphasis added). Why should we quote Scripture in the following way in a call to worship, then?

Thus says the Lord: "Let not the wise man glory in his wisdom, let not the mighty man glory in his might, let not the rich man glory in his riches; but let him who glories glory in this, that he understands and knows me, that I am the Lord who practice steadfast love, justice, and righteousness in the earth; for in these things I delight, says the Lord." (Jer. 9:23-24)

After all, it would be just as easy to switch from the singular to the plural and, without any substantive change of meaning at all, say:

Thus says the Lord: "Let not the wise glory in their wisdom, let not the mighty glory in their might, let not the rich glory in their riches; but let those who glory glory in this, that they understand and know me, that I am the Lord who practice steadfast love, justice, and righteousness in the earth; for in these things I delight, says the Lord."

Having decided what to say when giving a call to worship or benediction, one needs to determine *how* to say it. In dealing with this subject, it seems best to treat the call and the benediction separately since each has a unique place, content, and role in the liturgical proceedings. We shall deal first with the call.

We all know that the call to worship comes at the start of the service of worship. It is preceded, perhaps, only by an organ prelude or perhaps a prelude and an introit. As we have said, the purpose of the call is to focus the attention of the congregation on the object of worship, God. The call thus customarily consists of a biblical text or texts adapted for use in welcoming people to divine worship. The text asserts something about the nature of God, what God has done for us, and what God expects of us as we meet to listen to the word of God, to participate in the sacraments, and to offer praise and prayer. The leader in worship consequently should rise from his or her chair, and, with sensitivity to the mood set by the organ prelude or choral introit just concluded, move purposefully to the position from which the call is to be given. She or he should then look directly into the eyes of the congregation and begin.

Does this mean that the call to worship will need to be memorized? Often I think the answer is yes. At the very least it means that the call will have to be known well so that when the text clearly is intended directly for the congregation, eye contact with the congregation can be sustained. In fact the call to worship is typically spoken directly to the people who have come together to worship God. It therefore, as a rule, makes very little sense to look elsewhere than at them. In his book *Strong, Loving and Wise*, Robert Hovda makes the point that the person presiding at worship acts as a host for the gathered family of God. The host welcomes the family and, in that welcome, sets the tone for what is to ensue. What a strange welcome if the host is looking elsewhere than at those being welcomed! What a strange greeting if the one doing the greeting stares into a pulpit or lectern, or curiously fixes his or her gaze on a wall at the back of the room! The people gathered for worship are there in front of us who lead in worship. Thus, the focus of our attention, as we seek to focus the attention of the people on God, is the people themselves. They are our chief concern if our aim is to welcome them rightly.

There are times during a call to worship when the person giving the call may not reasonably be expected to look directly into the eyes of the congregation. One of those times is when the text being spoken clearly calls for the speaker's eye contact to be elsewhere. For example, the following words, obviously contituting a prayer to God, have been used as part of a call to worship.

> Blessed [are those whom you] choose and bring near,
>   to dwell in [your] courts!
> We shall be satisfied with the
>   goodness of [your] house,
>   [your] holy temple!
>
> (Ps. 65:4)

Because those words are the words of a prayer directed to God, the worship leader would avoid eye contact with the congregation. She or he would simply keep eye contact with the page, allowing the congregation the space to pray with the psalmist and the worship leader in the psalmist's words. However, before reading that text, it would be appropriate to look at the congregation and to call on the people to listen to what is about to be read. To do that, some such phrase as this could be spoken: "Hear these words from Psalm 65, verse 4." Once the reading of the text is completed, it would also be fitting, indeed warranted, to look into the eyes of the congregation and say, perhaps as follows: "Having heard these words of the psalmist, let us worship God."

The worship leader's direct speech to the congregation before and after the reading of the text of the psalm suits the psalmist's words to the liturgical moment in which they are being read. The words of the psalm itself, spoken not to the congregation but *for* it and to God in prayer, focus the attention of the congregation on the divine Presence in its midst. Additionally, by indirection, they indicate something of what God has done for the people and what God expects from them. It is the psalmist's and the worship leader's words together that constitute the call to worship. And, though the psalmist's words are not spoken directly to the people, eye to eye, the worship leader's are.

Another time the worship leader may not be looking directly at the congregation is when a responsive call to worship such as the following is being spoken. This call to worship is an adaptation of James 4:10, James 4:8, Psalm 122:1, and Psalm 18:24.

Leader: Humble yourselves before the Lord and the Lord will exalt you.

People: Draw near to God and God will draw near to you.

Leader: I was glad when it was said unto me, "Let us go to the house of the Lord!"

People: This is the day which the Lord has made; let us rejoice and be glad in it.

However, even here it is wise to make some contact with the people gathered for worship before starting the responsive reading of the text given above. For nothing is more debilitating to the movement into worship than a half-hearted, late, straggling entrance of the congregation at the start of a responsive call to worship. It therefore makes sense to ask the people to stand and get ready for the part they are to play in doing the call. The worship leader should look directly at the congregation and speak a sentence such as this one: "Please stand and join with me in the responsive call to worship printed in your bulletins." Once the people have stood and are prepared to begin, the worship leader can give the opening line of the text.

The benediction, like the call to worship, is spoken directly to the congregation. In fact, there is no reason ever to look anywhere else than right at the people to whom the benediction is being given. It is for them. As has been said, as God's people prepare to depart from worship, the benediction affirms for them what they most need to know. It affirms for them that the greatest blessing God can give is their blessing. The benediction promises the divine Presence itself in all of life, in high and mundane moments, in public and private affairs.

Often the benediction includes a reference to the Trinity. It reminds people that their fellowship with one another is grounded in the unity and fellowship of the Godhead. Thus, though the familial gathering at worship is about to end, no one leaves the sanctuary isolated or alone. Each leaves in company with God. Each leaves confident that what has been and will be required of God's people is being accomplished among them by God. God's people leave worship chastened, but supported, challenged, and empowered. Something of that truth therefore should come through to them as they receive the benediction. This is no time for the worship leader to appear staid, distant, and demanding! Rather it is a time or the worship leader to evidence his or her genuine concern for those about to go their separate ways. The worship leader's bearing, facial expression, gesture, and tone of voice should communicate both warmth and confidence, solicitousness and a genuine conviction that nothing "will be able to separate [people] from the love of God in Christ Jesus our Lord" (Rom. 8:39).

Some offer the benediction while making the sign of the cross over the community of worshipers. Others offer the benediction by raising the right arm and reaching out a hand over the heads of the members of the congregation. Still others reach out with both arms in a kind of wide, relaxed gesture of embrace. My own conviction is that the choice of gesture does not matter half so much as the way the gesture is carried out. Is it stiff and formal? Is it done with ease and a sense of gentle strength? If the gesture is done with ease and gentle strength, it will appear spontaneous, natural, suited to what is being said and to the purpose of the speaker or worship leader in saying it. If it appears awkward, effortful, and contrived, it will call attention to itself as a gesture and will not operate in a way consonant with the worship leader's intention.

It is good to remember that gestures need to be related to what has been called the speaker's center. This is the imaginary center of gravity of the human torso, located just below the sternum or breast bone, and at the solar plexus. This center is also thought of as the center of vulnerability. When you are standing tall and relaxed, the center seems to be exposed but not overexposed, and the feeling communicated is one of confident accessibility. When the center is overexposed, the feeling generated is one of defenselessness and weakness. When the center is tucked away behind hunched or arched shoulders or when it is turned away from the speaker's listeners, the feeling expressed is one of defensiveness.

Gestures "tied" to the center (elbows held in close to the rib cage), seem tentative, even timid, yet gestures that appear completely cut off from the center (elbows way out from the rib cage), may come across as gangly and lacking in purpose. The object with whatever gesture is being used in giving the benediction, then, is to have that gesture so related to the center that it appears purposive but not aggressive, strong but not tense, relaxed but not limp. The gesture may be extended to the congregation, but it is extended as from the worship leader's center, the very core of his or her person. In other words, the worship leader should not give the appearance of being detached from the gesture but rather caught up in it. The gesture is a movement of the self. It is an offering of the self.

To get a feel for what is right, assemble a group in the sanctuary of your church. Practice the gestures you will use in pronouncing the benediction, and let the group provide feedback on what is communicated to them by what you say and how you say it. If you do that, you may get a more objective "read" on your speech and gesture than it is possible for you to obtain on your own.

Before concluding this discussion of calls to worship and benedictions with some practice materials in the giving of benedictions, it seems appropriate to mention processionals and recessionals. There are times when worship leaders may be processing with the choir. Sometimes the processional occurs before the call to worship is given. When that is the case, the handling of the call to worship can be accomplished just as I have described it in this chapter. However, there are times when the call to worship is given *before* the processional. Similarly, the benediction may be given *after* the recessional. Then what do you do?

It is clear that you cannot look right into the eyes of the congregation if the congregation has its back to you! Even in this circumstance, however, you can speak the words of the call or benediction appropriately. The phrasing and emphasis can make sense. The tone of voice can be suited to the content being expressed. You can keep in mind to whom you are speaking (the congregation) and *for* whom you are speaking (Christ). And the purpose of the call or benediction can influence the way you give it. In fact, I would suggest that the call and benediction be spoken *as if* you were looking at the members of the congregation eye to eye, and that posture, facial expression, and gesture be handled as they would be handled in direct, face-to-face speech. If that is done, it seems likely that the voice will do what it is supposed to do and that the people will feel encouraged to respond fittingly to what is said.

Here are three benedictions, which may serve as models for you and which you may use as practice materials along with the calls to worship given earlier. In working with benediction #1, be sure you ask yourself what it means to be blessed and kept by God, what it means to have God treat you with kindness, to look on you with favor. Ask yourself what is distinctive about the peace of God. You might even jot down the connotations these words have for you so that God's blessing, protection, kindness, graciousness, favor, and peace have some personal significance. Then bring that personal significance to mind as you speak.

In benediction #2, remember that it is the grace of the *Lord Jesus Christ* and the love of *God* and the fellowship of the *Holy Spirit* that is being promised and secured for all. It is not just any old grace, any old love, any old fellowship. And in benediction #3 note the causal relationship between what precedes and what follows the comma. Notice, too, that the movement of the passage as a whole is toward the thought *"abound* in hope." Keep the passage alive, moving toward and generating expectation for that climax.

Benediction #1

The Lord bless you and keep you.
The Lord be kind and gracious to you.
The Lord look upon you with favor
and give you peace. Amen.

(Num. 6:24-26 adapted)

Benediction #2

The grace of our Lord Jesus Christ,
and the love of God, and the
fellowship of the Holy Spirit,
be with you all. Amen.

(II Cor. 13:14 adapted)

Benediction #3

May the God of hope fill you with all joy
and peace in believing, so that by the
power of the Holy Spirit you may
abound in hope. Amen.

(Rom. 15:13 adapted)

CHAPTER SIX

LEADING UNISON CONFESSION
AND RESPONSIVE PRAISE

Not all prayer and praise is spoken, obviously. Sometimes prayers and offerings of praise are sung by the congregation or by the choir or soloists, and certainly not all prayer and praise is rendered responsively or in unison. Often a pastor or worship leader may quote a doxological statement from Scripture or offer prayers on behalf of a congregation, speaking alone. Furthermore, there are times when only silence will do for either prayer or praise, the silence of the attentive and awe-filled heart.

Unison and responsive prayer and praise present pastors and worship leaders with peculiar speech communication problems, however. For that reason I will focus on such prayer and praise in this chapter. Plainly the discussion will have to be illustrative and suggestive rather than exhaustive and definitive. We will consider how to do one type of unison prayer, the confession of sin (together with the assurance of pardon). After that, we will discuss responsive readings from the psalter. These particular items present us with representative problems in the speaking of unison and responsive prayer and praise, and they are spoken by a good many Christians of various liturgical traditions Sunday after Sunday. First, the confession of sin and assurance of pardon.

Other than the Lord's Prayer itself, probably the most commonly spoken unison prayer is the corporate confession of sin. In the course of the church's history, this prayer, though not always and everywhere offered each Lord's day, has been offered in a variety of liturgical traditions with remarkable regularity. The reason for that, I think, is clear. In confessing our sin as a congregation gathered in Christ's name to worship God, and in beseeching God for forgiveness, restitution, and guidance, we bear witness to the fact that God is both holy and gracious, just and compassionate, demanding and supportive, the God of each of us and the God of all of us together.

We further acknowledge that what God expects of us can be achieved fully only as we are redirected in the conduct of our life again and again by God's own Spirit. In other words, we live not by our wits, but by God's wisdom. We are perfected, brought up to the "measure of the stature of the fulness of Christ" (Eph. 4:13), not in independence from God, but in dependence on God and on God's Word. The Word of God does not condone sin. It does not leave people contented with themselves as they are and with life as it is. Instead, the Word of God takes people as they are and presses them into the service of what God would have them be. It gives them a holy dissatisfaction with themselves and with the systems of common life and governance they have established or inherited. We confess our sins, that is to say, because we are a people of the Word.

Our confession is grounded in God's nature and will. It is not grounded in our human nature and our human will. It is not a response to feelings of guilt or shame or to a conviction that we somehow can be and therefore ought to be better people. Our confession of sin is part and parcel of our response to the gospel, God's Good News. So it is spoken in hope, not despair, in confidence, not anxiety.

Accordingly, our confession of sin is typically composed as follows: First there is a statement in which something of the nature of God is briefly set forth. This is followed by an admission that we have fallen short of the mark of God's will for us as disclosed in Christ and in Scripture. A plea for forgiveness ensues, followed by a petition in which God's help is sought for conducting our affairs in a manner more worthy of the calling we have received from Christ to live to the praise of God's glory. At last, the prayer as a whole is offered to God in Jesus' name. Notice how just such a pattern obtains in the following, slightly revised, classic confessional prayer.

Almighty and most merciful God; we acknowledge and confess that we have sinned against you in thought, word, and deed; that we have not loved you with all our heart and soul, with all our mind and strength; and that we have not loved our neighbor as ourselves. We ask you, O God, to forgive what we have been, to help us to amend what we are, and of your mercy to direct what we shall be; so that from now on we may walk in the way of your commandments, and do those things which are pleasing in your sight; through Jesus Christ our Lord. Amen.

Then, immediately following the completion of the unison prayer of confession, the assurance of pardon is given. In it the graciousness of God is affirmed and the benefits of God's forgiveness, proffered once for all in Christ, are appropriated by the worshiping congregation. The person leading in confession, paraphrasing passages of Scripture, may say, for instance:

Who is in a position to condemn? Only Christ, and Christ died for us, Christ rose for us, Christ reigns in power for us, Christ prays for us. (Rom. 8:34)

If anyone is in Christ, he or she becomes a new person altogether. The past is finished and gone, everything has become fresh and new. (II Cor. 5:17)

Friends: Believe the Good News of the gospel. In Jesus Christ we are forgiven. Amen.

Far from being downbeat, the prayer of confession, coupled as it always is with an assurance of pardon, is decidedly hopeful. It attests to God's faithfulness, and so it is itself an act of faith on the part of the church. It is a manifestation of the church's trust in God. Further, it is oriented toward the future, not the past. Its focus is not on things as they may have been with us or are with us. Rather its focus is on things as God would have them be. We confess our sin, in fact, precisely in order to turn from it toward God and toward the future God has secured for us in Christ. Our confession of sin is an act of repentance. Also, we do all this together as a church. We are not isolated and alone in our confession of sin and repentance. To the contrary, the confession and repentance of each of us is caught up in the unison confession of the people of God whom the Christ of God has called to be his own.

The trouble is that we often speak our prayer of confession as if all that has just been said were not true. One may hear the worship leader say, for example, "Let us make common confession of our sin to Almighty God." But then each person begins mumbling what is printed in his or her bulletin or worship book with little, if any, sense that what is being said is in fact the common confession of the church. Then, too, the mood may be decidedly downcast, the tone of voice weak and unexpectant, almost suggestive of a kind of spiritual groveling. Hardly a repentance filled with hope and trust in God! No wonder the assurance of pardon sometimes seems inappropriately sanguine! The congregation, preparing for the worst, suddenly has to adjust to Good News that sounds too good to be true, too easy. You've heard comments such as this: "It doesn't seem real to me. We confess our sins, receive a declaration of pardon, and then go out and do what we've always done, sort of like giving up on New Year's resolutions."

Why do people say such things? Why is their theology of confession so wide of the mark? Why does repentance appear to them to be exclusively their own business instead of God's business with them? Why does the forgiveness of God somehow come off as an indulgence of the wayward, a winking at sin instead of a costly defeat of it? Is it because catechetical instruction has somehow fallen through a crack in the sanctuary floor? Perhaps. Perhaps this, too, however: The way we lead our congregations in confession implies a theology of confession contrary to what we say we believe. If that is the case, then one step in the direction of helpful change is to correct our leadership.

Instead of mumbling our confessions from the chancel of the sanctuary, we can firmly and with full voice lead the congregation in a truly common confession of sin. Instead of giving our confession a tone of defeat and despair, we can give it a tone of solemn trust in God. And instead of reciting each phrase of our confession of sin lugubriously, we can speak with a heightened sense of expectation and movement. We can do that. And, if we do, it could be that our practice of confession might contribute to the renewal and transformation of our theology of confession.

This, too, needs to be said: The invitation must be of a piece with the confession itself, must not overwhelm it, and must not cause a hiatus in the movement of the service of worship as a whole. The invitation to confession is precisely an invitation, not a mini-sermon on why confession is needed; much less is it an apology for what is about to take place. As we move to confession, we do not need to be diverted by a sudden attempt to draw back up through that crack in the floor the catechetical instruction so long lost. Most prayer books, worship books, and directories of worship are clear on this point and offer helpful guidance in deciding what to say. What is recommended most commonly is a sentence or two from Scripture that indicates something of God's readiness to deal with our sin redemptively, or a simple statement such as, "Let us confess our sin to Almighty God."

Above all, the invitation to confession should be spoken while looking directly at the worshiping congregation. It should be said in an inviting, encouraging tone, not in an indifferent or scolding tone. We repent chiefly because "the kingdom of heaven is at hand" (Matt. 3:2). That is our primary motivation, not the anger of God or the threat of hell.

The following principles should therefore be kept in mind as we lead congregations in their unison confession of sin:

(1) The invitation to confession should be spoken directly to the people, eye to eye; and it should sound like an invitation and not a warning.

(2) The confession itself should be led in a clear, strong voice that helps the congregation to pray as one with expectancy, hope, and trust.

(3) The declaration of pardon should be confident and forthright, not guarded or tentative.

All this takes practice, so there follow here three additional prayers of confession together with invitations to confession and declarations of pardon. Keeping in mind the discussion just concluded, attempt to speak these invitations, prayers, and declarations in a way suited to their content and liturgical purpose.

In speaking the invitations to confession, be sure to look into the eyes of the congregation. In practice, of course, the congregation will be imaginary. Nevertheless, be sure you *see* it with your imagination, and let what you speak be an invitation, not a threat or demand. Anticipate the fact that, for the sake of spiritual renewal, the congregation just may want to confess its sin. Furthermore, harbor that same expectation concerning yourself. After all, as worship leader, you are not simply giving directions to others as if you had no need to follow them yourself. To the contrary, you are taking the lead in doing what the congregation itself is expected to do. The invitation to confession you speak is one you have expected, heard, and to which you intend to respond.

As for the declarations of pardon, I suggest that you memorize them. Keep in mind, however, that you are memorizing thoughts, their relationships to one another, and your purpose in speaking them. You are not simply committing to memory a string of words. Therefore, do not try to memorize each word in turn. Instead, memorize the declaration of pardon phrase by phrase, discovering each idea as if for the first time, and add each idea to the thought that has preceded it. By doing this you will establish the *progression* of thought. You will also find that the progression of thought, once firmly in mind, will help you recall the exact words you wish to speak. The crucial first step in memorization, therefore, is not reciting words in vain repetition but working out phrasing and emphasis according to the principles discussed and illustrated in chapters 3 and 4 of this book.

Now take a look at the prayers of confession themselves. In prayer of confession #1 observe how fully what is confessed—our "sinful nature," our "shortcomings and offences"—is grounded in the nature of God, who is "holy" and "merciful" and who knows us better than we can know ourselves. Similarly notice that, in prayer of confession #2, we confess our straying from the ways of God, our offences against God's laws, our doing of what we ought not to do, and our failure to do what we should, to a God who is at once "almighty" and "merciful" and who, in Christ, promises forgiveness to those who are penitent. Then, in prayer of confession #3, be aware that judgment against inhospitality and injustice, forgiveness of those sins and hope for a more just, kind, and humble life are provided by this same God, who here is particularly acknowledged to be righteous, compassionate, full of pity and mercy.

In other words, as you pray, remember that you are praying to God as God is known in Jesus Christ. You are not praying into thin air or into the void, and you are not drooping under the weight of some theological abstraction. Surely God is more than we can imagine, more than we can express in human terms, but God *is not less* than human, nor is God less than we can imagine. In a word, our unison prayer of confession must be led by one who understands and believes that, when we pray, we are speaking to God person to Person.

Prayer of Confession #1

Invitation: Let us join in confessing our sin to God.

Confession: Most holy and merciful God, we acknowl-
edge and confess before you our sinful nature, prone to evil and slow to do good, and all our shortcomings and offences. You alone know how often we have sinned, in wandering from your ways, in wasting your gifts, in forgetting your love. Yet, O God, we ask you to have mercy upon us who are ashamed and sorry for all we have done to displease you. Teach us to hate our errors; cleanse us from our secret faults; and forgive our sins; for the sake of your dear Son. And O most holy and loving God, help us, we pray, to live in your light and walk in your ways, according to the commandments of Jesus Christ our Lord. Amen.

Declaration of Pardon: Hear the Good News of the gospel!

The saying is sure and worthy of full acceptance, that Christ Jesus came into the world to save sinners.

He himself bore our sins in his body on the cross, that we might be dead to sin and alive to all that is good.

In the name of Jesus Christ, we are forgiven. Amen.

Prayer of Confession #2

Invitation: In penitence and faith, let us confess our sins to Almighty God.

Confession: Almighty and merciful God, we have erred and strayed from your ways like lost sheep. We have followed too much the devices and desires of our own hearts. We have offended against your holy laws. We have left undone those things which we ought to have done and we have done those things we ought not to have done. O Lord, have mercy upon us. Spare those who confess their faults. Restore those who are penitent, according to your promises declared to the world in Jesus Christ our Lord. And grant, O merciful God, for his sake, that we may live a holy, just, and humble life for the glory of your holy name. Amen.

Declaration of Pardon: Almighty God, who freely pardons all who truly are repentant, now fulfill in every contrite heart the promise of redeeming grace, remitting all our sins and cleansing us from an evil conscience, through the perfect sacrifice of Christ Jesus our Lord. Amen.

Prayer of Confession #3

Invitation: Let us make common confession of our sin to Almighty God.

Confession: O God of righteousness and compassion, who looks with pity on those who have nowhere to lay their heads, and who condemns inhospitality and injustice wherever they are found, of your mercy, condemn all inhospitality and injustice among us. Forgive us our sin. Grant us true repentance. And guide us by your Word and Spirit in the way of Christ, that we may do justice, love kindness, and walk humbly with you, our God. This we ask in Jesus' name and for his sake. Amen.

Declaration of Pardon: Friends, hear this Good News.

If we confess our sins, God is faithful and just, and will forgive us our sins and cleanse us from all unrighteousness.

I declare to you, in the name of Jesus Christ, we are forgiven. Amen.

Having discussed how to lead in the unison confession of sin, I would now like to attend to the issue of leadership in the responsive reading of passages from the book of Psalms or the psalter. As I do so, let me say that some of what is mentioned in these next several paragraphs is applicable to the reading of the Scriptures generally. Likewise, what is said especially at the beginning of chapter 7, "Reading the Scriptures: Theory and Practice," is applicable here. Customarily, however, psalter selections have a unique place in the liturgy of the church, distinct from the reading of Old Testament, Gospel, and Epistle lessons. Further, because they are so frequently spoken responsively, separate treatment of them at this point seems warranted; for it is precisely the matter of *responsive* reading that I want to go into.

In different liturgical traditions what is to be read from the psalter is determined by a variety of criteria. Among them are these: particular days of the Christian or civil year, specific occasions (for example, the ordination of a person to the ministry of Word and sacrament), and specific subject matter. In those traditions that make regular use of the common lectionary, a particular psalm is designated for each Lord's day throughout the year, just as is the case with Old Testament, Epistle, and Gospel lessons. No matter what the method of selection, however, virtually all Christian folk do make fairly regular use of passages from the psalter in their services of worship.

The psalter, or the book of Psalms, contains the gamut of human emotion, from exhilaration to despair, from praise of God to anger with God. It contains songs of the individual soul in rapture and confession, in danger and flight, in ease and comfort. It contains songs for the nation and songs for the people of God. It contains liturgical hymns. It also contains poetic instruction in wisdom, in the fear of God, and in right living. Many of the psalms are exquisitely beautiful and extol the beauties of creation and of holiness and the divine beauty itself. Others betray the ugliest of human motives—vengefulness, a vaunting nationalism, spiritual pride, even bloodlust.

All that is human, from the heights to the depths, from the profound to the banal, is hauled before God in the Hebrew-Christian songbook, the psalter. Nothing is hid from our own eyes or from God's. In the psalter, with God, we see ourselves at our best and at our worst. But above all, as scholars have said, in the psalter we can hear the voice of humanity reaching out to God; yet we believe that reaching out itself is by inspiration of God. We believe it is the prompting of God's Spirit within us as individual human beings and as a community of faith. So the songs of the psalter are not just our songs, they are the songs of the Holy Spirit as well.

We sing them, we chant them, we perform them antiphonally with choirs, soloists, and congregations. We read them together in unison and sometimes we read them on our own. Sometimes we give them a solo rendering.

It is true that some of the psalms lend themselves more easily to one type of reading than another. Psalm 24, for example, is clearly written for antiphonal performance, probably by two choirs. Psalm 139, on the other hand, is just as clearly the desperate cry of one solitary individual seeking God's deliverance from enemies, from murderers. It is an individual lament.

Yet, for all the compositional variety of the psalms, and despite the many ways we have of expressing them in worship, one of the most common methods of performance, if not the most common, is the method of responsive reading. It therefore behooves us to pay some attention to further developing our ability to lead responsive readings from the psalter. I say *lead* advisedly, for what often happens in the responsive reading of the psalter is that the leader fails to lead. She or he fails to give the congregation anything to which it can actually respond. Instead, as W. J. Beeners once put it, it all comes down to this: "I'll take a line, then you take a line." The congregation and the worship leader then alternate lines, but not much else is shared. The sense and significance of what is being said are not probed. The words of the psalm may get spoken, but the human drama the words are meant to evoke gets lost.

The psalms themselves would not have that happen, if they could help it. For the psalms, in large part, are composed according to the constraints of a unique poetic technique that combines thought, feeling, and form and that does not allow for their convenient separation. That poetic technique is called parallelism. The most common types of parallelism are these: (1) Synonymous Parallelism (a parallelism that achieves intellectual and emotional intensity through creative repetition):

> The Lord answer you in the day
>   of trouble!
> The name of the God of Jacob
>   protect you!
> May [God] send you help from the
>   sanctuary,
>   and give you support from Zion!
> May [God] remember all your offerings,
>   and regard with favor your burnt
>   sacrifices!
>
> (Ps. 20:1-3)

(2) Antithetical Parallelism (a parallelism that achieves intellectual and emotional intensity through contrast):

> Many are the pangs of the wicked;
>   but steadfast love surrounds [those]
>   who [trust] in the Lord.
>
> (Ps. 32:10)

(3) Constructive Parallelism (a parallelism that achieves intellectual and emotional intensity through depicting the appropriate consequences or further development of a line of action or thought):

I cry aloud to [you] Lord,
    and [you answer] me from [your] holy hill.

(Ps. 3:4)

(4) Climactic Parallelism (a parallelism that achieves intellectual and emotional intensity through adding detail and enhancing or expanding a particular thought, attitude, or mood):

O sing to the Lord a new song;
    sing to the Lord, all the earth!
Sing to the Lord, bless [God's] name;
    tell of [God's] salvation from day to
        day.
Declare [God's] glory among the nations,
    [God's] marvelous works among all
        the peoples!
For great is the Lord, and greatly
    to be praised;
    [the Lord] is to be feared above all gods.

(Ps. 96:1-4)

The basic literary technique of the psalms not only contributes to a holding together of sense and significance or intellectual and emotional content. The various psalms are clearly intended to evoke, to awaken, to call into being in us certain types of experiences: lamentation, praise, thanksgiving, an identification with the history of God's people, an adherence to divine wisdom, trust in God—just to name a few! That means that the psalms are designed for rhetorical or persuasive effect. The authors of the psalms intend to secure the imaginative involvement of the reader in what they write, for it is only through such imaginative involvement that the experiences depicted in the psalms can be evoked. We are not to admire or criticize the psalms from a distance, and we are certainly not to give them a dispassionate rendering, to embalm them and put them on view. Instead we are to engage the psalms so that they become living literature for us. We are to find resonance in our souls for what the psalms are about. In fact, we are to *know* the way of the psalms as God knows the way of the righteous (Ps. 1:6). That is not mere head knowledge! That is intimate, full, embodied knowledge! In brief we are to be moved by the psalms as the divine itself is moved by the caring and the cares of those with whom it is most closely associated.

Certainly if that is to happen for the congregation, the respondents in our responsive readings from the psalter, it must happen first and foremost in those who lead. Not only will those who lead need to work out the details of phrasing and emphasis as they were discussed in chapters 3 and 4, they will also have to work out an understanding of the thematic and dramatic development of the psalm to be read. They will have to know what kind of human experience is at the heart of it and how that human experience is portrayed. They will have to come to grips with the intellectual content and with the perspective governing the treatment of that content. And they will have to adjust to the shifting moods implicit in the psalmist's treatment of that content. They will have to know the whole psalm and not just their own part. And as part of their preparation for leading in a responsive reading, they will have to speak the whole psalm through until it becomes part of them, for they will need to anticipate the response of the congregation. Indeed, they will need to set the stage for the congregation's response by the way they themselves deliver their own lines.

Scholars in the field of the rhetorical analysis of literature have argued that every literary passage has an intended, ideal audience or listening and performing congregation. It is up to the leader in a responsive reading or performance of a psalm, therefore, to join league with the text in creating out of the actual congregation an ideal congregation, a congregation ready to be moved as the text would have it be moved, a congregation sympathetic to the concerns of the text and resonant with its life.

In preparing passages from the psalter for responsive reading, the worship leader would find it helpful to ask himself or herself the following questions:

(1) What is the theme of this psalm? Is it lament? Is it praise? Is it the articulation of divine wisdom?

(2) From what vantage point or vantage points does the psalmist expect me to get involved with the theme?

(3) Are there shifts in mood and in the way the psalmist treats the theme? If so, where are those shifts and how should I identify with them?

(4) What type of parallelism predominates in the psalm? Is there any variety in parallelism? How may the variety in parallelism be related to the shifting of perspective or mood, or to the manner of treating the theme?

(5) How do I find myself responding to this psalm as I perform it? Do I find myself resisting anything it has to say to me or anything it apparently wants to do with me? Further, why am I resisting? For example, do I find that what the psalm has to say is abhorrent to me or that it is in some way intimidating? What can be done to overcome my resistance at least for the duration of the psalm's performance?

(6) Does my performance of the psalm seem to express, as fully as I am able to express it, my best understanding of it and my involvement with its life?

(7) Does my performance of the leader's part alone appear to give the congregation something to which it can respond with its own lines? That is, as far as I can tell, is my rendering of the leader's lines accurate, interesting, and suggestive?

Answering questions such as these, of course, does not guarantee a meaningful responsive reading of a psalm in a service of worship. However, it does guarantee that the worship leader has taken some pains to prepare the reading and to do the most responsible job she or he can do.

It is important to prepare the congregation for its role in the responsive reading of the psalms also. Of course one cannot stop the service of worship in mid-flight in order to do this, yet there are steps that can be taken to help the congregation build its competence in responsive reading. For one thing, those preparing services of worship can publish in advance in their church newsletters not only Old Testament, Gospel, and Epistle lessons and texts for sermons, but psalter selections as well. This will provide an opportunity for members of the congregation to study the psalter before they speak it. Thus at least some will be saved from the faltering that frequently occurs when people are sight-reading.

Then, too, there is no reason why catechetical instruction

of young people and new adult members cannot include workshops dealing with church members' responsibilities in worship. Of course it is important to provide some basic information concerning the history and theology of worship and the sacraments, but it is important as well to give attention to the order of worship, its form and content, and how the different parts of the service are conducted. If this is done, actual practice in unison prayer and praise, and the singing of hymns and responsive readings of the psalter can be undertaken. Today there is great stress on lay involvement in worship. This is as it should be. That involvement could be improved, however, to everyone's delight! Why not empower people to carry out the responsibilities assigned to them? Why not strive for greater *quality* as well as greater *quantity* of lay participation in worship? Why not assist people in building further the skills they need to do their work? After all, that is the meaning of the word *liturgy*. Its origin is the Greek *leitourgia* (the work of the people).

Another thing that can be done to educate people in how to do responsive readings—and, for that matter, unison readings of prayers of confession and affirmations of faith as well—is to include such instruction in occasional catechetical preaching. It is my conviction that biblical preaching is the norm in the worship of the church, yet that does not entirely exclude topical preaching, catechetical preaching, and so forth. In fact, it requires it in order that, among other things, people will know what biblical preaching is and why it is done. So why not have a series of sermons sometime dealing with worship? And why not include in that series practical instruction and guided experiences in the responsive reading of psalms?

Finally, work with your choir! After all it is the purpose of the choir to assist the congregation in doing what it is supposed to do. The choir is not there for entertainment. It is there to inspire and guide congregational singing, congregational unison reading, and congregational responsive reading. The choir is a talented, trained extension of the congregation. In a way it is the congregation's vanguard. Ask the choir director for maybe five minutes of rehearsal time now and then to go over the responsive reading so that at least some worshipers are thoroughly prepared for the role they are to play. Or go over the responsive reading of the psalter with your choir director and let him or her train the members of the choir. Make the choir your ally in leading worship.

There now follow three psalms laid out for responsive reading. Study these psalms. Speak them through fully. Ask yourself at least some of the seven questions enumerated in my discussion of the worship leader's preparation of psalms for responsive reading. Certain of the questions, after all, may seem more pertinent to you than others, given the particular psalm being considered and your reaction to it. Speak the psalms again until you are satisfied that you are expressing as completely as possible your best understanding of them. Then try speaking the worship leader's lines only while hearing in your mind, as it were, the anticipated responses of the congregation. The congregation's lines are italicized. The leader's lines are not. These readings, by the way, are taken from the psalter as translated in the Episcopal *Book of Common Prayer* (New York: Seabury Press, 1979, with minor adaptations and adjustments for responsive reading).

Notice that the responses in Psalm 1 and Psalm 146 complete the thought initiated by the leader. These are responsive readings you definitely will want to go over with your choir. If you don't , the meaning of the psalms may be lost. Each congregational response must be "discovered" and given as a completion of the leader's line. Thus, done correctly, the responsive reading of psalms 1 and 146 can be exciting. It can almost have the feel of poems being composed in the moment of their utterance. Done incorrectly, however, the aesthetic beauty, dramatic movement, unity and sense of the psalms can be lost. Psalm 90 is a bit easier even though the congregation's lines are longer. This is so because, all the way through, both the leader's and the congregation's lines express complete thoughts.

Responsive Reading #1

Happy are they who have not walked in the counsel of
    the wicked,

*Nor lingered in the way of sinners, nor sat in the seats of the
     scornful!*
Their delight is in the law of the Lord,
     And they meditate on that law day and night.
They are like trees planted by streams of water,
     Everything they do shall prosper.
It is not so with the wicked;
     They are like chaff which the wind blows away.
Therefore the wicked shall not stand upright when
     judgment comes,
     Nor the sinner in the council of the righteous.
For the Lord knows the way of the righteous,
     But the way of the wicked is doomed.
                                                    (Ps. 1)

Responsive Reading #2

Lord, you have been our refuge from one generation to
     another.
     Before the mountains were brought forth,
          or the land and the earth were born,
          from age to age you are God.
You turn us back to the dust and say, "Go back, O child
     of earth."
     For a thousand years in your sight are like yesterday
          when it is past and like a watch in the night.
You sweep us away like a dream; we fade away
     suddenly like grass.
     In the morning it is green and flourishes;
          in the evening it is dried up and withered.
For we consume away in your displeasure;
     we are afraid because of your wrathful indignation.
     Our iniquities you have set before you,
          and our secret sins in the light of your countenance.
When you are angry, all our days are gone;
     we bring our years to an end like a sigh.
     The span of our life is seventy years,
          perhaps in strength even eighty;
          yet the sum of them is but labor and sorrow,
          for they pass away quickly and we are gone.
Who regards the power of your wrath?
     Who rightly fears your indignation?

    So teach us to number our days
      that we may apply our hearts to wisdom.
Return, O Lord; how long will you tarry?
    Be gracious to your servants.
    Satisfy us by your loving-kindness in the morning;
      so shall we rejoice and be glad all the days of our life.
Make us glad by the measure of the days that you afflicted us
    and the years in which we suffered adversity.
    Show your servants your works
      and your splendor to their children.
May the graciousness of the Lord our God be upon us;
    prosper the work of our hands;
    Prosper our handiwork.

                                    (Ps. 90)

Responsive Reading #3

Hallelujah!
Praise the Lord, O my soul!
    I will praise the Lord as long as I live;
      I will sing praises to my God while I have my being.
Put not your trust in rulers, nor in any child of earth,
    For there is no help in them.
When they breathe their last, they return to earth.
    And in that day their thoughts perish.
Happy are they who have the God of Jacob for their help!
    Whose hope is in the Lord their God;
Who made heaven and earth, the seas, and all that is in them;
    Who keeps promises forever;
Who gives justice to those who are oppressed,
    And food to those who hunger.
The Lord sets the prisoners free;
    The Lord opens the eyes of the blind;
      the Lord lifts up those who are bowed down;
The Lord loves the righteous; the Lord cares for the stranger;
    The Lord sustains the orphan and widow,
      but frustrates the way of the wicked.
The Lord shall reign for ever,
    Your God, O Zion, throughout all generations
      Hallelujah!

                                  (Ps. 146)

CHAPTER SEVEN

READING THE SCRIPTURES:
THEORY AND PRACTICE

Many books have been written on the subject of the oral performance of literature, and more than a few of those books have considered effective reading of the Scriptures. It is not my intention to rehash what has been said in those books. Nevertheless, some theoretical exploration is necessary before we deal with the practice of Bible reading in worship. The theoretical exploration is needed because, just as was the case in our study of how to do calls to worship and benedictions, and how to lead prayers of confession and responsive readings, the reading of the Scriptures needs to be understood as an act of interpretative-situational speech. To read a passage from the Bible correctly, that is to say, one has to develop some understanding of it and of how to express that understanding accurately. Then, too, one has to be sensitive to the physical and liturgical setting in which the expression takes place. This sensitivity is required so that the worshiping congregation may be encouraged to respond appropriately to the passage being read.

To some people all this may be self-evident, yet others may object, feeling somehow that the reading of the Scriptures should not be treated just like the reading of anything else. The Bible, after all, is sacred literature, not grist for some performance mill. To paraphrase a statement in the Presbyterian *Confession of '67*, the Bible is the unique and authoritative witness to Jesus Christ in the church universal and God's Word to us. So some argue, "We don't want the Bible interpreted. We want it read straight. We don't want any imposition of the personality of the reader on the text or on us who are listening. We think that would interfere with the work of the Spirit in interpreting God's Word to our hearts." Some think that it is not the job of readers to demonstrate mastery of the text, or to demonstrate how talented they are at getting and holding our attention. They say, "Just speak the words clearly and sensibly; don't try to suggest attitude or point of view."

That may not be particularly well said, but it is said forcefully and sincerely often, and not without cause. There are a number of people, perhaps you are among them, who are put off by what appears to them to be bad acting from the lectern or the pulpit. They feel embarrassed by what they see and hear. For whatever reason, the reader seems to get in the way of what is read. She or he seems to loom over the text, to dominate it. These listeners would just as soon that the reader "backed off," giving less of self and more of the passage.

It is possible to give a shoddy performance of a passage of Scripture. It is possible to loom over a text, to dominate it. It is possible to embarrass a congregation by drawing attention to yourself as you read. Consequently, excessively egocentric and idiosyncratic readings of passages from the Bible no doubt are better discouraged than indulged.

However, the idea that we can somehow read a passage "straight," giving it without interpreting it, without suggesting attitude or point of view, and without having any sense of how listeners may respond to it as it is read, also needs to be discouraged. That idea needs to be discouraged because it simply is not true. Neutrality is also an interpretation. It is the purveying of an attitude or mood. And objectivity is a carefully considered, established, and maintained point of view meant to set the perspective out of which the words of a text are not only spoken, but also heard. Together neutrality and objectivity say, "Hands off! Let's not get too involved with this thing."

And it's a question, isn't it, whether neutrality is a warranted response to everything in Scripture. And it is a highly debatable assumption that the appropriate point of view for speaking an Old Testament narrative or a parable of Jesus or a selection from the writings of the apostle Paul is one of studied objectivity. More of that later when we delve into attitude and point of view in the handling of specific biblical texts. For now, it is sufficient to observe that one cannot use those basic principles of phrasing and emphasis discussed in chapters 3 and 4 without at least engaging a passage intellectually, trying to get and communicate the sense of it. And to engage a passage intellectually, to try to make sense of it for yourself and others when you read it, is to interpret it.

Thus there is no way just to say words or to speak ideas without suggesting how people are to hear and respond to those words and ideas. No, the reading of anything, including the reading of the Scriptures, is a complex rhetorical act in which text, reader, listener, and setting inevitably interact with one another and influence one another. Consequently, like all other speech communication efforts in leading worship, reading the Scriptures is an act of interpretative-situational speech.

The reader's task is to see to it that in the interaction and mutual influence of text, reader, listener, and setting, nothing and no one gets slighted. In other words, he or she must make every effort to see to it that the interaction and mutual influence are facilitated with integrity. That takes careful preparation, obviously, and requires a clear under-standing of what is going on when the Scriptures are being read in a service of worship.

What is going on? Well, for one thing, the grace of God is being manifested. The words of Scripture are very human words. I don't think anybody seriously doubts that. Nevertheless, God's Spirit, given in the church to inspire, guard, and guide its life, has made and continues to make divine use of the Bible's human speech. Christ Jesus, you will recall, remarked: "You have heard that it was said to the [people] of old . . . , but I say to you . . ." (Matt. 5:21-22). And so, by the Spirit, he exercised authority over the words of Scripture. No less does Christ, by that same Spirit, exercise authority over the scriptural word today. He does with Scripture what he will to make of us what God wills. The human speech of the Bible consequently is more than merely human speech. It is divine speech, too. It is what God's Spirit has to say to us in order that we may be more than just our own kind of human being.

The reading and hearing of the Scriptures is a means of grace. With the Bible's words God addresses us personally in

Christ, establishes a point of contact between us and the divine self, breathes into our tired lungs the breath of a new life, and fashions a people of God. That is why, before the reading of the Scriptures, we pray in Christ's name for the illumination of the Holy Spirit. And only then do we say, "Let us hear the Word of God."

The reason for rejecting the idea of attempting to give a straight, uninterpreted, nonrhetorical reading of the Scriptures thus rests not only in the nature of the speech communication process itself. It rests also in the nature of the divine Word. Apparently God does not disparage the self-evidently human speech of the Bible, but rather takes it up just as it is, claims it as a divine possession, and uses it to accomplish a divine purpose. So who are we to attempt to hold the words of Scripture at a distance, to render them with calculated objectivity and neutrality? Who are we to wrest a pale, liturgical recital from the Bible's blood and guts? It is not for us to diminish the range of human expression in which God apparently delights. To the contrary, it is for us to speak it and to hear it: the rage of the abused, the cry of the destitute, the self-assertions of the defiant, the foolish, the ungodly. All are to be given voice with our voices. All are to be given a hearing with our ears.

In addition to the fact that the grace of God is manifested when the Scriptures are read in worship, we also have the fact of the manifestation of the church. What I mean by that is that what God's Word does when it is read and heard—and preached, of course—is to form and reform the church. The response to the Word when it is read is not just the aggregate of our individual, subjective reactions. It is also the unison response of the people the divine has called to be its own. It is the response of a particular congregation of the church. Christ's Spirit, which interprets the words of Scripture to our hearts, is not the private possession of the individual, meant to inspire, guide, and guard his or her life in isolation from all other lives. Instead, that Spirit is God's gift to the church to inspire, guide, and guard its life for the sake of the world, in order that a witness may be perpetuated in the world concerning the world's true end and ultimate good.

Further, the response to the Word provoked by the Spirit is

to be as full as the word itself. It is to be a response of heart, soul, mind, and strength. Rhetorically speaking it is logical, ethical, and emotional, not logical only. It is the response of the entire being of the body of Christ, the church. As a result, those who lead in worship, who read the Scriptures and respond to them under the inspiration and guidance of the Spirit, are called on to respond as the congregation as a whole responds. They are called on to respond to the Scriptures with all their heart, soul, strength, and mind. They are called to respond with their whole being. In the final analysis, the question for the reader of Scripture is not this: Do I interpret this passage for the congregation as I read it or do I attempt to refrain from any interpretation? Instead, the questions are: Am I interpreting this passage responsibly? Am I responding to it appropriately? Am I attending to it with my whole being? And am I therefore leading the people of God in this act of worship as God would have me lead them?

Of course, errors will be made. Perhaps even sins will be committed. But let them be conscientious, not inadvertent errors, and let them be sins of commission, not omission. Let them be "brave" sins, as Martin Luther might call them, sins in any case forgivable, errors redeemable by the grace that attends the reading and the hearing of God's Word. So, do we prepare and practice readings of Scripture before we give them? Certainly we do lest, as Paul Scherer once put it, "We give the impression that the words have gone in at our eyes and come out at our mouth without ever having passed through our mind," or, I might add, our soul.

Having explored some theoretical issues concerning the reading of the Scriptures in worship, we now move on to consider some very practical matters: first, how to introduce and conclude the reading of Old Testament, Gospel, and Epistle lessons. I mention this principally because this is sometimes done with very little attentiveness to the movement and pace of worship as a whole. In other words, the liturgical setting for the reading of the Scriptures now and then is given short shrift. In the case of introductions, it is almost as if the directed movement of worship is halted so that a mini-homily on the text may be given prior to reading it. Or one sometimes gets a rather rambling delivery of background information, a smattering of historical facts, coupled with a synopsis of the text and its literary context. By the time the reader gets around to the text itself, it seems anti-climactic!

Now there may be times when the historical or literary setting—or both—are so crucial to an intelligible hearing of the text that some background, introductory information must be given. If that is the case, I can only say, prepare! Give the background material pointedly and succinctly, and so word and deliver it that it whets the appetite of the listener for the scriptural passage coming up. Don't steal the Bible's thunder! However, I suspect you will find that such preparatory remarks are rarely needed. It is amazing how much intelligibility can be given to a reading when that reading itself is carefully thought through and practiced.

More commonly a passage will be introduced with any one of a number of liturgical formulas that may be said with expectancy and with the speaker's eyes focused directly on the congregation. For example:

> The Old Testament reading is from the book of Jeremiah, chapter 1, verses 1 through 10. Hear the Word of God.

Or:

> The holy gospel of our Lord Jesus Christ according to Luke, chapter 1, verses 46 through 55.
> *With the congregation responding:*
> Glory to you, O Lord.

Or:

> A reading from Paul's letter to the chuch at Rome, chapter 8, verses 31 through 39. Hear God's Word.

As for words concluding the reading from the Scriptures, they may be as simple and direct as these, spoken with energy and with the reader's eyes on the congregation:

> So ends the reading from God's holy Word, and to God's name be glory and praise.

Or:

The Word of the Lord.
With the congregation responding:
Thanks be to God.

What one does *not* need to say is, "May God add a blessing to the reading of this holy Word," as if that Word itself were not God's blessing!

As for actually reading the Scriptures themselves, a number of things need to be said. First, as I have indicated in the theoretical section of this chapter, inevitably one must decide what attitude or attitudes a passage of Scripture seeks to evoke in the reader and the listener. I use the word *attitude* instead of "mood" or "feeling tone" because it suggests not only inward response, but outward response as well. It has as much to do with posture and even facial expression as it has to do with any inner state of being. You can feel words of adoration, praise, thanksgiving, and conviction almost straighten your spine, can't you? The center is elevated, expansive. The sensation is one of holding the head high. The eyes are bright and alive. The cheek bones seem to rise almost as in a smile, but not quite. As dancers say, the body appears to rise out of the shoes.

Think of that great ascription of praise in the third chapter of Ephesians: "Now to [the One] who by the power at work within us is able to do far more abundantly than all that we ask or think, to [that One] be glory in the church and in Christ Jesus to all generations, for ever and ever. Amen" (vv. 20-21). Surely as you think such thoughts and as you say them, you can't let your chin drop, your shoulders droop, your jaw hang, your eyes go dull. You can't let your center cave in and your weight crash down upon the arches of your feet as if to break them! No, Paul's ascription kindles a contrary attitude of bouyancy, of lift.

But likewise it would be absurd to hold such an attitude when the content of your speech changed. If you were reading, for instance, these words of Paul:

O foolish Galatians! Who has bewitched you, before whose eyes Jesus Christ was publicly portrayed as crucified? Let me ask you only this: Did you receive the Spirit by works of the law, or by hearing with faith? Are you so foolish? Having begun with the Spirit, are you now ending with the flesh? Did you experience so many things in vain?—if it really is in vain. Does [the One] who supplies the Spirit to you and works miracles among you do so by works of the law, or by hearing with faith?   (Gal. 3:1-5)

Would you not need to identify with Paul's frustration, with his eagerness to open up himself to his listeners so that they might open up to him, have their memories stirred and their consciences pricked? And if you did so identify with Paul's intent, would that not be reflected on your face and in your posture as you said his words? You can almost feel the air go out of the lungs, the rib cage collapse, the sternum fall as the thought is expressed: "O foolish Galatians!" Then an urgency arises that lifts the center a bit and moves it toward the listener as if to invade that listener's space with Paul's redirection of his own thought: "Let me ask you only this: Did you receive the Spirit by works of the law, or by hearing with faith?" Then perhaps there is even more urgency, more intensity, more ironing of the spine as the rhetorical questions—the answers to which should be self-evident to the Galatians—heap up: "Are you so foolish?" etc.

Attitude identification and attitude shift, both as inward response and as physical bearing and facial expression, thus are inevitable. They are inevitable because they mark transitions in the thought that is being perceived and expressed by the reader. Further, as listeners see these attitudes embodied in the reader, their own involvement with the content of the passage is quickened. Covertly their muscles tense and relax with the reader's, and with mind and body they find the experience of the passage coming alive in their own persons. This is the very definition of empathic response, to "feel into" another's situation. In the reading of the Scriptures, empathy is the reader's and listener's "being with" each other and with what is being read.

I offer the following two selections from Scripture as exercises in identification of attitude and attitude shift. You will find that both require subtlety and range. In the first passage, the shifts in attitude all happen within the one character who speaks, Paul, with whom the reader is to identify. In the second passage the shifts in attitude come to different characters: Jesus, the narrator, the crowd, and the inhabitants of Jerusalem. But all of those shifts still occur within the narrator, with whom the reader is to identify. The narrator, that is, suggests what others in the story are experiencing as he or she describes their actions or quotes them. It is not unlike what any one of us would do quite spontaneously in conversation if we spoke about an incident of great interest to us. We would mention who did what and who said what, and in doing so we would suggest each character's attitude without trying actually to impersonate anyone.

You may discover that you will need to work through these exercises in identification of attitude and attitude shift more than once or twice before you are able to match your inner perception of attitude to an outward expression of it. You may find that you discover a number of different ways of understanding and expressing each shift. Why not explore several of the options before settling on those you feel are most appropriate? Perhaps you will even find in the end a certain measure of frustration because not all of the valid possibilities you discovered can be shared in a single reading. Good! No reading is perfect, complete. No reading can exhaust the possibilities of a given biblical text.

Exercise #1 in Identification of Attitude and Attitude Shift

If I speak in the tongues of [human beings] and of angels, but have not love, I am a noisy gong or a clanging cymbal. And if I have prophetic powers, and understand all mysteries and all knowledge, and if I have all faith, so as to remove mountains, but have not love, I am nothing. If I give away all I have, and if I deliver my body to be burned, but have not love, I gain nothing.

Love is patient and kind; love is not jealous or boastful; it is not arrogant or rude. Love does not insist on its own way; it is not irritable or resentful; it does not rejoice at wrong, but rejoices in the right. Love bears all things, believes all things, hopes all things, endures all things.

Love never ends; as for prophecies, they will pass away; as for tongues, they will cease; as for knowledge, it will pass away. For our knowledge is imperfect and our prophecy is imperfect; but when the perfect comes, the imperfect will pass away. When I was a child,

I spoke like a child, I thought like a child, I reasoned like a child; when I became [an adult], I gave up childish ways. For now we see in a mirror dimly, but then face to face. Now I know in part; then I shall understand fully, even as I have been fully understood. So faith, hope, love abide, these three; but the greatest of these is love.   (I Cor. 13:1-13)

Exercise #2 in Identification of Attitude and Attitude Shift

When [Jesus and the disciples] drew near to Jerusalem and came to Bethphage, to the Mount of Olives, then Jesus sent two disciples, saying to them, "Go into the village opposite you, and immediately you will find an ass tied, and a colt with her; untie them and bring them to me. If any one says anything to you, you shall say, 'The Lord has need of them,' and he will send them immediately." This took place to fulfil what was spoken by the prophet, saying,

> "Tell the daughter of Zion,
> Behold, your king is coming to you,
> humble, and mounted on an ass,
> and on a colt, the foal of an ass."

The disciples went and did as Jesus had directed them; they brought the ass and the colt, and put their garments on them, and he sat thereon. Most of the crowd spread their garments on the road, and others cut branches from the trees and spread them on the road. And the crowds that went before him and that followed him shouted, "Hosanna to the Son of David! Blessed is he who comes in the name of the Lord! Hosanna in the highest!" And when he entered Jerusalem, all the city was stirred, saying, "Who is this?" And the crowds said, "This is the prophet Jesus from Nazareth of Galilee."   (Matt. 21:1-11)

We have discussed and worked with attitude, one of the primary concepts involved in the effective reading of the Scriptures in worship. Another basic concept, also mentioned in the theory portion of this chapter, is point of view. Point of view has to do with the basic frame of reference for engaging the experience depicted in a text of Scripture. The form of the passage itself provides a clue to what that point of view or frame of reference is. For example, in an Epistle lesson, the point of view the reader has to take is the one provided by the author of the text. We need to discover that author's voice. We need to concern ourselves with how the author seems to identify with what is talked about in the text. If we are to read a passage from Romans, for example, we need to orient ourselves to the subject matter in the way Paul, the letter writer, would have us orient ourselves.

Or take a biblical book such as the letter to the Hebrews. We do not know who the actual author is. Nevertheless, we can feel that author's presence. And if we are to read a passage from Hebrews responsibly, we need to attempt to see all that is discussed in the book the way the author would have us see it. We also need to speak what we see from that vantage point or point of view.

Or if we are reading a psalm, much the same kind of effort needs to be made to see all that is being presented in the psalm from the standpoint of the person who was responsible for the psalm's composition. Then we need to read the psalm sustaining that point of view so that our listeners, the worshiping congregation, may also be led through all the "ins" and "outs" of the psalm as the psalmist would have them be led. By establishing a defensible (I will not say correct) point of view, by locating a passage's central voice, we give our reading coherence. Despite the subtle, varied, and sometimes far-ranging changes in attitude that may be found in the text, the text, as read and heard, possesses unity.

We can demonstrate the way a point of view gives coherence to the reading of a passage of Scripture by discussing the performance of Psalm 139. First, read the edited version of the psalm, which has found some popularity in the psalter sections of certain often used hymnbooks:

Edited Version of Psalm 139

O Lord, thou hast searched me and known me!
Thou knowest when I sit down and
    when I rise up;
Thou discernest my thoughts from afar.
Thou searchest out my path and my lying down, and
    art acquainted with all my ways.
Even before a word is on my tongue, lo,
    O Lord, thou knowest it
    altogether.

Thou dost beset me behind and
     before, and layest thy hand upon me.
Such knowledge is too wonderful
     for me; it is high, I cannot attain it.
Whither shall I go from thy Spirit?
Or whither shall I flee from
     thy presence?
If I ascend to heaven, thou art there!
If I make my bed in Sheol, thou
     art there!
If I take the wings of the morning
     and dwell in the uttermost parts of
     the sea, even there thy hand shall lead me,
And thy right hand shall hold me.
If I say, "Let only darkness cover me,
     and the light about me be night,"
Even the darkness is not dark to thee,
     the night is bright as the day;
     for darkness is as light with thee.
How precious to me are thy thoughts,
     O God! How vast is the sum of them!
If I would count them, they are more
     than the sand. When I awake, I am still with
     thee.
Search me, O God, and know my
     heart! Try me and know my thoughts!
And see if there be any wicked way
     in me, and lead me in the way everlasting.

The psalmist in that edited version of Psalm 139 gives us a
perspective or point of view that is basically sanguine even if
it is not completely agreeable. There are some clashing
attitudes to interrupt the awe and wonder and acclaim of
God. For instance, if all were well, why would the psalmist
ever say, "Let only darkness cover me"? Then, too, despite
the generally upbeat and confident tone of the work, there is
that reference at the end of the psalm to a "wicked way"
contrasted with "the way everlasting."

In the unedited version of the psalm contained in holy
Scripture, however, the point of view is anything but
sanguine! The psalmist is in dreadful circumstances. He or
she is "up against the wall," surrounded by enemies,
murderers, God-haters. And if God does not come to the

defense of the psalmist, all is lost. So the psalm is a fierce lament, a crying out to God in utter desperation. It is not a paean of praise simply acknowledging God's omniscience and admitting the humble state of the psalmist. There is even rage here as the psalmist seeks deliverance from oppressors. The psalmist's, the author's, predicament and point of view—his or her voice, if you will—are set in verses 19 through 22, "O that thou wouldst slay the wicked, O God." From that point of view, all of the earlier statements about the wonder, mystery, and knowledge of God are made. And from that point of view, the concluding petition, "Search me, O God. . . . and lead me in the way everlasting," is offered. The following is Psalm 139 in its entirety. As an exercise in establishing and maintaining point of view while still expressing various attitudinal shifts, attempt the reading of this psalm. Give yourself time before you begin to imagine yourself in the predicament of the psalmist, upset with God, fearful about your circumstances, anxious for vindication, deliverance, retribution.

Exercise #1 in Establishing and Maintaining Point of View

O Lord, thou hast searched me and known me!
Thou knowest when I sit down and when I rise up;
   thou discernest my thoughts from afar.
Thou searchest out my path and my lying down,
   and art acquainted with all my ways.
Even before a word is on my tongue,
   lo, O Lord, thou knowest it altogether.
Thou dost beset me behind and before,
   and layest thy hand upon me.
Such knowledge is too wonderful for me;
   it is high, I cannot attain it.

Whither shall I go from thy Spirit?
   Or whither shall I flee from thy presence?
If I ascend to heaven, thou art there!
   If I make my bed in Sheol, thou art there!
If I take the wings of the morning
   and dwell in the uttermost parts of the sea,
Even there thy hand shall lead me,
   and thy right hand shall hold me.

If I say, "Let only darkness cover me,
  and the light about me be night,"
even the darkness is not dark to thee,
the night is bright as the day;
for darkness is as light with thee.

For thou didst form my inward parts,
  thou didst knit me together in my mother's womb.
I praise thee, for thou art fearful and wonderful,
  Wonderful are thy works!
Thou knowest me right well;
  my frame was not hidden from thee,
when I was being made in secret,
  intricately wrought in the depths of the earth.
Thy eyes beheld my unformed substance;
  in thy book were written, every one of them,
the days that were formed for me,
  when as yet there was none of them.
How precious to me are thy thoughts, O God!
  How vast is the sum of them!
If I would count them, they are more than the sand.
  When I awake, I am still with thee.

O that thou wouldst slay the wicked, O God,
  and that [people] of blood would depart from me,
[people] who maliciously defy thee,
  who lift themselves up against thee for evil!
Do I not hate them that hate thee, O Lord?
  And do I not loathe them that rise up against thee?
I hate them with perfect hatred;
  I count them my enemies.
Search me, O God, and know my heart!
  Try me and know my thoughts!
And see if there be any wicked way in me,
  and lead me in the way everlasting!

Up to this point our discussion of point of view in reading
the Scriptures has focused on texts that feature only one
speaker, the author. Such texts are said to be written in the
lyric voice. This simply means that there is only one voice or
character for the reader to worry about. The other type of
literature you find in the Scriptures, however, is literature
written in the so-called epic voice. Such literature features
not one voice but two or more, not one character but several

perhaps, plus a narrator. In all this complexity, you need to keep in mind that it is the narrator who provides the perspective or point of view out of which the story is told and from which all the characters are portrayed.

Most of the time this narrator is a conventional, third-person omniscient storyteller. That means that the narrator is not part of the story, does not speak as one of the characters of the story. Instead the narrator speaks from outside the story as one who has a privileged and comprehensive knowledge of the characters and of the story line or plot. In fact, the narrator controls the characters and the plot, controls the unfolding of the story, determines how the story will begin, reach a climax, and end.

It does not necessarily follow that the narrator's point of view is one of neutrality, however. Far from it! The narrator has an ax to grind, has a point to make, so the narrator works directly on those to whom the story is being narrated, wins their interest, and helps them follow the action of the story. The audience for the story attends to the story on the narrator's terms.

To read a biblical narrative well, therefore, you have to assume the position of storyteller yourself. There is no other option. *You* have to give life to the characters. *You* have to express their varying attitudes and points of view. *You* have to control the pacing of the story, the unfolding of the plot. *You* have to convey your keen interest in the story to those who are listening. And *you* have to determine which details and characters need to be highlighted as the story unfolds.

Plainly that means that you will need to study the story, live with it a while before you read it to others. You will need to get into the mind of the narrator as fully as you can until you can believe yourself telling the story. Finally there may be no determining whether your reading of the biblical narrative is "correct," for stories have a way of capturing the imaginations of people differently. But you can achieve a *responsible* reading, one that takes the fullest possible account of the details of the text, and you can achieve a *good* reading, one that is lively, not dull, profound and not trivial. You can achieve a reading that reflects your best understanding of the kind of person who is telling this story and why she or he is doing so.

The following narrative passage from the book of II Kings is a second exercise in establishing and maintaining point of view. See if you can imagine yourself in the storyteller's shoes. Note particularly the narrator's fascination with ironic contrasts and turns: Naaman, for example, "was a mighty man of valor, but he was a leper." A "little maid" from the land of Israel has confidence in the God of Israel and in Elisha, God's prophet. The king of Israel, however, does not. Naaman comes "with his horses and chariots" to Elisha's house, but the prophet doesn't even bother to come out. He sends a servant. Naaman is "fit to be tied" when he is told to "wash" and "be clean" in the Jordan. Yet his servants—the not-valorous, the not-powerful, the not-wise-and-renowned—save him from his foolish pride. Perhaps these ironic contrasts, twists, and turns suggest what the narrator's point of view might be and what is to be gained by telling the story. What do you think?

Exercise #2 in Establishing and Maintaining Point of View

Naaman, commander of the army of the king of Syria, was a great man with his master and in high favor, because by him the Lord had given victory to Syria. He was a mighty man of valor, but he was a leper. Now the Syrians on one of their raids had carried off a little maid from the land of Israel, and she waited on Naaman's wife. She said to her mistress, "Would that my lord were with the prophet who is in Samaria! He would cure him of his leprosy." So Naaman went in and told his lord, "Thus and so spoke the maiden from the land of Israel." And the king of Syria said, "Go now, and I will send a letter to the king of Israel."

So he went, taking with him ten talents of silver, six thousand shekels of gold, and ten festal garments. And he brought the letter to the king of Israel, which read, "When this letter reaches you, know that I have sent to you Naaman my servant, that you may cure him of his leprosy." And when the king of Israel read the letter, he rent his clothes and said, "Am I God, to kill and to make alive, that this man sends word to me to cure a man of his leprosy? Only consider, and see how he is seeking a quarrel with me."

But when Elisha the man of God heard that the king of Israel had rent his clothes, he sent to the king, saying, "Why have you rent your clothes? Let him come now to me, that he may know that there is a prophet in Israel." So Naaman came with his horses and chariots, and halted at the door of Elisha's house. And Elisha sent a messenger to him, saying, "Go and wash in the Jordan seven times, and your flesh shall be restored, and you shall be clean." But Naaman was angry, and went away, saying, "Behold, I thought that he would surely come out to me, and stand, and call on the name of the Lord his God, and wave his hand over the place, and cure the leper. Are not Abana and Pharpar, the rivers of Damascus, better than all the waters of Israel? Could I not wash in them, and be clean?" So he turned and went away in a rage. But his servants came near and said to him, "My father, if the prophet had commanded you to do some great thing, would you not have done it? How much rather, then, when he says to you, 'Wash, and be clean'?" So he went down and dipped himself seven times in the Jordan, according to the word of the man of God; and his flesh was restored like the flesh of a little child, and he was clean.   (5:1-14)

Perhaps you have discovered by now that what is crucial to handling attitude shifts and to establishing a point of view or governing perspective or centering voice in the reading of a passage of Scripture, is the ability to imagine in concrete detail the experience the text is meant to evoke. This is hard work because the text is distant from us by whole epochs of human history. We simply do not have the psalmist or the narrator or the biblical letter writer with us. We do not know how the original teller of the Naaman story would have sounded. We cannot reproduce the voice of the psalmist, and we have never heard Paul. We can base our understanding on a careful study of the text's details, and we can use the expertise provided by scholarly commentary as we do so. But if these authors, these storytellers, letterwriters, and psalmists, are to come alive for us and through us for others, we will have to find, in our own experiences, feelings, or attitudes, ways of looking at things that at least are roughly analogous to those provided in the text. And we will have to use these to inform our speech. We will have to make use of what actors and fine singers call "sensory memory."

Let me illustrate. Very few of us, perhaps none of us, have been in dire straits just like those of the psalmist who cried out, "O that thou wouldst slay the wicked, O God" (Ps. 139:19). But we have read about, heard about, or seen on television or in the movies situations full of oppression, danger, violence, and murder. The movie *Platoon*, which depicted senseless mayhem during the Vietnam war, certainly was filled with such. And couldn't you imagine some of those Vietnamese villagers whose homes were burned and whose children were killed, crying out to God with something approaching the terror and rage of the psalmist? And couldn't you imagine U. S. soldiers doing the same? And couldn't you imagine yourself crying out to God because of the apparent senselessness of it all and because of your inability to do anything about it?

If you want to give us the psalmist's voice as you read Psalm 139, if you want to provide for us the perspective out of which all that is said in that text is to be heard and experienced, and if you want to take us through the attitude shifts provided in the text, you will have to enter again that circumstance of frustration which inspired your own cry to God. You will have to make the psalmist's cry your cry. You will have to remember and relive the effects your cry to God had on your own person. Every muscle in your body, from toe tip to tongue tip, will have to quiver with that cry. And if your cry is subdued or silent, that only means that the muscular strain will be greater. Sensory memory, you see, means just that: the effects of experiences on your senses. Or, to put it another way, the cry of the psalmist and your cry have physicality. They have neuro-muscular effects. Don't shun those effects. Indulge them.

All speech is motivated by change. The discovery of a new idea changes you. The discovery of a fresh attitude changes you. The appropriation of an author's point of view, his or her way of dealing with the ideas and attitudes expressed in a text, changes you. Let that change, whether great or small, superficial or profound, be manifested in your body, on your face. For that physical gesture is vital for securing your listener's empathy. Then, in the next millisecond after the physical gesture is given, give the vocal gesture. Say the words that clear up for the listener what has happened to you. That way the experience of the text will be vibrant and alive for all concerned with it, for you the reader, and for your listeners, the worshiping congregation.

So far in talking about Scripture reading we have dealt with how to get into the experience of a text in order to make it real for others. Now in concluding our discussion let's turn to the subject of eye contact.

One thing that is asked again and again with regard to the reading of the Scriptures is, What do I do with my eyes? Is it appropriate to look at the congregation while reading a passage or not? If it is appropriate to do so, when should I look up and for how long? I'm sure you've seen instances when eye contact appeared to be completely inappropriate, even embarrassing. At other times it may have helped you appreciate what was being spoken. As with most other matters having to do with effective speech communication in leading worship, there are no tricks of the trade to get readers off the hook of responsibility for making their own judicious decisions. On the other hand, there are some principles that may prove useful in making those decisions. One of those principles may be stated this way: *Quality* of eye contact is more important than *quantity* of eye contact.

Playing "peek-a-boo" with the congregation is not high quality, meaningful eye contact. Merely glancing up now and then between phrases will not do the job. If you do look up from the page while reading, there needs to be a reason for doing so, and that reason needs to be self-evident. For instance, if you look at the congregation, it should be because what is being spoken is meant specifically for them. If you look up from your text but not directly into the eyes of the congregation, that is, if you use what is commonly called "indirect eye focus," it should be because your mind's eye is riveted on a thought or image. In a word, one does not pretend to make eye contact either with the congregation or with ideas or mental pictures. On the contrary, one really makes contact, and one does so because one feels the need to do so. Eye contact, like all other aspects of body language including posture and facial expression, results from honest involvement with content and a desire to share that content.

A second principle to help readers decide whether to use direct or indirect eye contact or to keep contact with the text may be stated as follows: If you wish to look up from a text while reading it you need to be *free to do so*. You have to know a passage well if you are going to take your eyes off the page. In fact, the reason meaningless, peek-a-boo eye contact is so common is that some people think they should make a connection with the congregation whether or not they are really prepared to do so. Not trusting themselves away from the page for more than half a second, however, they quickly blink back down to it so as not to lose their place. I suggest, therefore, that what can be more important than eye contact is the "readability" of the reader's face. If the congregation can see the face of the reader, if the reader's head is up enough from the page to allow for that, and if the reader is standing back far enough from the lectern to allow members of the congregation to feel that they have access to him or her despite that lectern, eye contact may not always be absolutely necessary. You can get by without it. What is crucial is that the reader be deeply involved with his or her reading, identifying shifts of attitude and responding to them, establishing point of view and maintaining it. If those things are not happening, eye contact will not count for much, and even a memorized and recited passage will seem underprepared, artificial, inauthentic, and awkward.

A third principle, and the most important principle for determining what to do about eye contact while reading from the Scriptures, is this one: What readers do with their eyes depends on what is going on in the passage they are reading. For example, if you are reading a psalm that in its entirety is a personal prayer to God, it makes no sense at all to look at the congregation. The congregation is overhearing the prayer, is perhaps even praying the prayer with and through the reader whom the congregation sees as identified with the author of the text. Frankly, the more direct the link between the experience of the author and the experience of the congregation, the more indirect the connection between the reader and the congregation. The reader is giving expression to the experience of the author. He or she is voicing the author's prayer. He or she is standing before the congregation in the author's stead. Thus the prayer printed on the page becomes more fully the prayer of the congregation if the reader does not look at the congregation, but looks at the text or else focuses on ideas and images contained in the text.

On the other hand, as was mentioned earlier, in a narrative

passage the reader takes the position of the storyteller. The storyteller does not talk to characters in his or her story. Rather the storyteller's connection with them is indirect. If I am telling you a story as part of a conversation I am having with you, I will look at you most intensely when I am giving straight narration. If I start to quote a character in my story, however, I will look away from you. I will avert my eyes and suggest rather that I am looking at other characters in the story, for the characters within the story talk to one another. It is only the narrator who talks to the audience. So if you look up at the members of a congregation while reading a biblical story to them, you will do so on the narrator's lines. When you speak character's lines, on the other hand, you will use indirect eye focus or simply look at the page.

In certain cases, of course, such as in the reading of an Epistle lesson or certain psalms, the text may call for both direct and indirect eye contact in addition to straight reading with your eyes on the page. Even if all the ideas in a text are intended directly for the congregation, that is to say, the reader would not be expected to sustain relentless, eyeball-to-eyeball contact with the congregation. No one does that even in an informal chat. When talking to people informally, we look at them now and then, hold focus on them for a time. Then we look away from them. We give ourselves some space to get into our thoughts, and we give our listeners space to deal with what we have said. Likewise, in reading certain psalms and virtually all Epistle lessons, we may look at the page a good deal of the time, look away from the page some of the time in order to focus indirectly on the thoughts we are expressing, and now and then look directly at those who are listening to us.

For practice in this matter of eye focus or eye contact while reading Scripture, I have selected the following Old Testament, Gospel, and Epistle lessons from Cycle A of the Common Lectionary, the Eighteenth Sunday After Pentecost. In order to give you some idea of how to handle eye contact in these passages, I have had them printed in this way: Regular print indicates that you should keep your eyes on the page. CAPITAL LETTERS INDICATE THAT YOU SHOULD LOOK DIRECTLY AT THE CONGREGATION.

Italicized print indicates that you may wish to use indirect eye focus, looking away from the page but focusing on thoughts and images and not on your listeners.

Now the frequency of use of direct and indirect eye contact will vary from reader to reader depending on his or her knowledge of the text, response to the text, and degree of speaking ease in the liturgical setting. Eye contact need not be established at every point in the text where it can be justified. What I have done, therefore, is mark these passages for a fairly limited amount of eye contact, which I feel most readers can handle even if they have not had a lot of experience in reading the Scriptures in worship. If you feel you can justify and use more than is indicated, please consider youself free to do so. The first of these passages features very slight editorial changes to facilitate the use of at least somewhat more sex-inclusive language.

Eye Contact Exercise # 1

Seek the Lord while the Lord may be found, CALL UPON THE LORD WHILE THE LORD IS NEAR; let the wicked forsake their way, and the unrighteous their thoughts; let them return to the Lord, that the Lord may have mercy on them, AND TO OUR GOD, FOR GOD WILL ABUNDANTLY PARDON. "For my thoughts are not your thoughts, neither are your ways my ways," SAYS THE LORD. "For as the heavens are higher than the earth, so are my ways higher than your ways and my thoughts than your thoughts. For as the rain and the snow come down from heaven, and return not thither but water the earth, making it bring forth and sprout, giving seed to the sower and bread to the eater, so shall my word be that goes forth from my mouth; it shall not return to me empty, but it shall accomplish that which I purpose, and prosper in the thing for which I sent it." [SO SAYS OUR SOVEREIGN GOD.]
(Isa. 55:6-11 adapted)

Eye Contact Exercise # 2

For to me to live is Christ, and to die is gain. If it is to be life in the flesh, that means fruitful labor for me. *Yet which I shall choose I cannot tell.* I am hard pressed between the two. My desire is to depart and be with Christ, for that is far better. BUT TO REMAIN IN THE FLESH IS MORE NECESSARY ON YOUR ACCOUNT. Convinced of this, I know that I shall remain and continue with you all, FOR YOUR PROGRESS AND JOY IN THE FAITH, so that in me you may have ample cause to glory in Christ Jesus, because of my coming to you again. ONLY LET YOUR MANNER OF LIFE BE WORTHY OF THE GOSPEL OF CHRIST, so that whether I come and see you or am absent, I may hear of you that you stand firm in one spirit, with one mind STRIVING SIDE BY SIDE FOR THE FAITH OF THE GOSPEL. (Phil. 1:21-27)

Eye Contact Exercise # 3

The kingdom of heaven is like a householder who went out early in the morning to hire laborers for his vineyard. After agreeing with the laborers for a denarius a day, HE SENT THEM INTO HIS VINEYARD. And going out about the third hour he saw others standing idle in the market place; and to them he said, "You go into the vineyard too, and whatever is right I will give you." SO THEY WENT. Going out again about the sixth hour and the ninth hour, he did the same. AND ABOUT THE ELEVENTH HOUR HE WENT OUT AND FOUND OTHERS STANDING; and he said to them, "Why do you stand here idle all day?" They said to him, "Because no one has hired us." He said to them, "You go into the vineyard too." AND WHEN EVENING CAME, the owner of the vineyard said to his steward, "Call the laborers and pay them their wages, beginning with the last, up to the first." And when those hired about the eleventh hour came, EACH OF THEM RECEIVED A DENARIUS. Now when the first came, they thought they would receive more; BUT EACH OF THEM ALSO RECEIVED A DENARIUS. And on receiving it they grumbled at the householder, saying, "These last worked only one hour, and you have made them equal to us who have borne the burden of the day and the scorching heat." BUT HE REPLIED TO ONE OF THEM, "Friend, I am doing you no wrong; did you not agree with me for a denarius? Take what belongs to you, and go; I choose to give to this last as I give to you. Am I not allowed to do what I choose with what belongs to me? Or do you begrudge my generosity?" SO THE LAST WILL BE FIRST, AND THE FIRST LAST. (Matt. 20:1-16)

CHAPTER EIGHT

ADMINISTERING BAPTISM AND
SERVING COMMUNION

Because it would be utterly beyond the scope of this book on effective speech communication in leading worship to investigate all the issues involved in the theology and practice of baptism and communion, I have decided to focus on one subject. In brief, I am focusing on our leadership in the celebration of the eucharist or Lord's Supper and on baptism as an act, Christ's act and our act in the church. I am focusing on the doing of the sacraments and more specifically on what the person presiding in worship does.

By now we realize that the spoken word in worship is never a matter of words alone. It is a matter of words and deeds, of vocal and physical gesture. It is a matter of embodied discourse. And if that is true in the giving of calls to worship and benedictions, in the speaking of unison prayer and responsive praise, and in the reading of the Scriptures, it is even more obviously true when we baptize persons or serve communion. As far back as the fourth century, Augustine of Hippo referred to the sacrament of communion as the visible Word, as the Word of God seen, done, accomplished. Certain sixteenth-century scholars, both Roman Catholics and reformers, also stressed God's Word as deed or action among us. Erasmus, for example, preferred to think of Christ himself not as *verbum* but as *sermo*, not as Word of God in some static sense of that term, but as rhetorical, persuasive, sermonic act. The reformer, John Calvin, too, emphasized the concept of the Word as something enacted, done. And John Knox made the doing of the Word the very heart and soul of his understanding of communion, the Lord's Supper. He would have us focus not so much on the communion elements themselves as on the taking, breaking, sharing, and eating of the bread, and the pouring out and drinking of the wine. Words spoken, water sprinkled or poured, bread broken and eaten, wine poured out and drunk, all together constitute the sacramental signs of God's presence and activity.

The Word proclaimed in the reading and preaching of the Scriptures and the Word proclaimed in the sacraments of baptism and communion thus are one and the same Word of God. God speaks. Yet, in speaking to us, God also acts to accomplish what is spoken about. By the Word-Act of God, we are made part of the community of faith through baptism. And by the Word-Act of God, we are consecrated and nourished in the communion of saints as we eat bread and drink wine in remembrance of Christ till he comes.

It should not surprise us to discover, then, that John Calvin, for one, insisted that the reading of the Scriptures, preaching, and the observance of the sacraments should always be held together. For they belong together. To express it in perhaps too mundane a figure, they are the two sides of the one coin of God's Word. It is not that God's Word is only audible in the reading of the Scriptures and preaching and only visible in the sacraments. No, it is rather this: That while, in the reading and preaching of the Word, audibility is stressed, in the conduct of the sacraments, visibility and physicality are stressed. In reading and in preaching, physical gesture helps to reinforce and interpret the vocal gesture, which is primary.

In the case of the sacraments, however, it appears to be just the reverse. In the sacraments physical gesture is primary while vocal gesture helps to reinforce and interpret that physical gesture. It becomes quite clear, I think, if you try to imagine participating in a baptismal or eucharistic liturgy while simply listening to the service with your eyes shut or hearing the service performed on audiotape. A sermon at least makes sense when you can't see the preacher. In fact, a sermon can even make sense when you can't hear the preacher. I have read sermons silently with profit. But if you cannot see or in any way physically take part in a sacramental action, that action makes precious little sense. A sacramental action, for the most part, is quite clearly a gestural, kinesthetic, tactile experience.

Certainly the Scriptures bear witness to the unity of word and deed in reading, preaching, and sacramental action in the liturgical life of the early church. In Acts chapter 2 for instance, following the outpouring of the Spirit on Jesus' disciples, Peter preaches a mighty sermon in which the saving acts of God in Christ are depicted. Particular attention is given to Jesus' death, resurrection, and ascension, and to his sending of the Holy Spirit in fulfillment of the promise spoken by John the Baptist and recorded in Luke 3:16: "I baptize you with water; but . . . he will baptize you with the Holy Spirit and with fire." Following the sermon, so we are told, those who received Peter's word were baptized and were made part of the fellowship of the church, where they "devoted themselves to the apostles' teaching and fellowship, to the breaking of bread and the prayers" (Acts 2:42).

Similarly, in Luke 24:13-35, the story is told of the risen Jesus' encounter with two disciples on the road to Emmaus. Downcast, confused, dispirited, the disciples not only failed to recognize who Jesus was, they likewise failed to see any meaning in the recent events of Jesus' passion. So Jesus, "beginning with Moses and all the prophets . . . interpreted to them in all the scriptures the things concerning himself" (24:27). Then later, at table, Jesus "took the bread and blessed, and broke it, and gave it to them. And their eyes were opened and they recognized him" (24:30-31). The recognition came with the gestural, kinesthetic, tactile experience of the breaking of the bread following Jesus' preaching. It came as a response to the Word-Act of God made known through the recitation and interpretation of the Scriptures and through the sacramental action undertaken by Jesus.

Scripture reading, preaching, and sacramental actions, then, are all means of grace given to the church at its inception in order that its experience of the Word-Act of God in worship might be complete. In the reading of the Scriptures and preaching, the Word-Act of God is proclaimed. And, as Paul seems to suggest in his first letter to the Corinthians, that proclamation becomes a living sermon in the sacramental action of the church (I Cor. 11:26). To repeat, that does not mean that the reading and preaching of the Scriptures is all word and no deed, is all sound and no motion, is all a matter of hearing and not in any way a matter of seeing. Nor does it mean that sacramental action is all deed and no word, is all motion and no sound, is all seeing, touching, tasting, smelling and not hearing. Instead it means that the word is primary in Scripture reading and preaching whereas the deed is more focal in sacramental action. And, consequently, it also means that you cannot fully experience the one without the other, the spoken word without the enacted word, the enacted word without the spoken word. Without the reading of the Scriptures and preaching, sacramental action is robbed of its full significance. Yet, without any sacramental action at all, ever, the proclamation of the Word is left incomplete. In the economy of our worship, word and sacrament belong together, just as in the economy of the divine self-disclosure, speech and act are one.

For the presider at the observance of the sacraments, this oneness of word and deed, this suiting of the action to the word and the word to the action, with particular focus on action, means that three things need to be given very careful attention. First, in handling the spoken portions of the sacramental liturgy, care must be taken to ensure that, as nearly as possible, the full intellectual and emotional content of the liturgical texts is realized in expressing them. They must never become mere words. They must never be recited as if their sense and significance could be communicated completely apart from the presider's understanding and appropriation of them. The presider must pay attention to problems of phrasing and emphasis, attitude and point of view, subject matter and purpose just as she or he must do with the reading of the Scriptures or other liturgical texts. And the presider must take care to embody the thought she or he is trying to express. The presider's face and body need to be as alive to the text's meaning as his or her mind and voice.

Let me illustrate. Suppose you were beginning a service of baptism with this scriptural affirmation:

All authority in heaven and on earth has been given to me. Go therefore and make disciples of all nations, baptizing them in the name of the Father and of the Son and of the Holy Spirit, teaching them to observe all that I have commanded you; and lo, I am with you always, to the close of the age.   (Matt. 28:18-20)

It is obvious, I think, that those words are meant as a commandment to the whole church. They are confident, authoritative, sweeping. There is no hedging. There is no hesitancy. There is a threefold dramatic movement to the passage, a beginning, middle, and end. The beginning: "All authority in heaven and on earth has been given to me." The middle: "Go therefore and make disciples of all nations, baptizing them in the name of the Father and of the Son and of the Holy Spirit, teaching them to observe all that I have commanded you." The end: "And lo, I am with you always, to the close of the age." The attitude is one of boldness. The point of view is that of one issuing a challenge and taking the lead in undertaking that challenge. So the tone of voice is full, the center is up, alive, expansive. The face is responsive to every nuance of thought. There is discovery of thought. There is progression of thought to a climax. And there is denouement or resolution.

Therefore, to read or speak such a passage without "getting into it," without in some measure at least trying to live up to its expressive demands, would be to misread it. You could even ask yourself what it would be like to speak those words appropriately to a congregation of thirty, of one hundred, of five hundred, or a thousand. If you did that, you might get a feel for what would be required in order to give the text a suitable rendering in varied worship settings.

Or suppose, in a communion service, you were speaking the words of institution as they are recorded in Paul's first letter to the Corinthians:

I received from the Lord what I also delivered to you, that the Lord Jesus on the night when he was betrayed took bread, and when he had given thanks, he broke it, and said, "This is my body which is for you. Do this in remembrance of me." In the same way also the cup, after supper, saying, "This cup is the new covenant in my blood. Do this, as often as you drink it, in remembrance of me." For as often as you eat this bread and drink the cup, you proclaim the Lord's death until he comes.   (11:23-26)

Here again the commandment is to the whole church. But it is more instructional than assertive, more reflective, less vital and energetic than the baptismal passage quoted earlier. Yet it too has a beginning, middle, and end, a progression of thought that needs to be expressed. It is not static just because it is reflective. The beginning: "I received from the Lord what I also delivered to you." The middle: "That the Lord Jesus on the night when he was betrayed took bread, and when he had given thanks, he broke it, and said, 'This is my body which is for you. Do this in remembrance of me.' In the same way also the cup, after supper, saying, 'This cup is the new covenant in my blood. Do this, as often as you drink it, in remembrance of me.' " The end: "For as often as you eat this bread and drink the cup, you proclaim the Lord's death until he comes."

One's pacing and use of pause would need to reflect that movement of thought. That would be necessary so that the listener could follow the progression of thought in the passage and respond to it rightly. And the discovery and development of thought would likewise need to be expressed in the speaker's attitude or bearing, in his or her point of view or identification with the purpose of the passage, and in facial expression and eye focus. Failing that, the words of institution would simply be misquoted almost as if other words had been substituted for them.

For if words are to be spoken right, they must be spoken with appropriate vocal and physical gesture. They must be seen as well as heard. They must be treated as *sermo* not *verbum*, as rhetorical act and not as dead letter. Or, to come back to the place where we started this discussion, the handling of the liturgical texts associated with the sacraments requires the same kind of sensitivity to interpretative and situational dynamics as is required for effective speech communication in leading worship generally.

The second thing that needs to be remembered in handling the sacraments is that the coordination of eye contact and gesture with the spoken word is more critical than at any other moment in the conduct of worship. This is because so many different types of texts are being dealt with, and they

are directed sometimes to the whole congregation, sometimes to single groups of people gathered in front of the
congregation, sometimes to individuals, and sometimes to
God. Furthermore, as one speaks, one is often called on to
allude to the physical elements that play such a vital role in
sacramental observances. One alludes to the water of
baptism, to the bread and wine of communion, to the table
upon which the elements of the eucharist are placed. And all
of this happens before the act of baptism itself is engaged in
and before the breaking of the communion bread, the
pouring of the communion wine, and the offering of the
bread and cup to the people.

Besides the scriptural warrants for the sacrament of
baptism such as the one quoted earlier, for instance, there are
words of instruction that interpret the meaning of the
sacrament for those immediately involved in it and for the
congregation as a whole. Clearly such passages should be
known so well that they can be spoken directly to the people
with a considerable amount of sustained eye contact. One
would definitely hope not to have to play peek-a-boo with
words such as these:

Obeying the word of our Lord Jesus, and confident of his promises,
we baptize those whom he has called.

In baptism God claims us, and puts a sign on us to show that we
belong to God. God frees us from sin and death, uniting us with
Jesus Christ in his death and resurrection. By water and the Holy
Spirit, we are made members of the church, the body of Christ, and
joined to Christ's ministry of love, peace, and justice. Let us
remember and rejoice in our own baptism, as we celebrate this
sacrament.

I am not saying that such instructional passages would
have to be entirely memorized, though that indeed might be
desirable. I am saying that such passages would require
careful preparation in order for one to determine where
direct eye contact was most essential. The speaking of these
passages would have to be practiced, too, so that direct eye
contact could be managed with facility.

In baptism there are also questions directed to those being

baptized or to their parents. In addition, sometimes those being baptized have a sponsor who is charged with the responsibility of helping facilitate the development of faith and spiritual nurture of the new Christian. In such cases, these persons have questions directed to them as well. A very real problem of communication is to state these questions in such a way that they are both personal and public, the peculiar business of those being addressed yet no less the business of those who are witnesses to the baptism. Surely you would want to look straight at a person standing before you for baptism when you said words such as these: "Do you desire to be baptized?" And you would want to speak loudly enough to be heard by everybody and to encourage the respondent to give a full-voiced reply. Yet just as surely you would not want your contact with the person answering your question to be cold and indifferent, formal, or still worse, intimidating. Rather, you would hope to communicate your happiness that the person is there and ready to say, "I do."

And what about the question-and-answer format for the congregational declaration of faith using the words of the Apostles' Creed? That has certainly been a crucial part of the baptismal service in many traditions since ancient times. Would you not want to face the congregation eye to eye when you said, "Do you believe in God the Father? Do you believe in Jesus Christ, the Son of God? Do you believe in God the Holy Spirit?" And would you not desire so to communicate your intentions in tone of voice and facial expression that the congregation's response in articulating its faith might appear to be expected, desired, sought after?

Or when you were saying a prayer of thanksgiving to God over the water of baptism, might you not wish to reach out and touch the water as you said, "By the power of your Spirit, bless this water . . . "? In fact, you might not wish to do so. If you did wish to touch the water, however, if that seemed to you to be a meaningful liturgical action, you would have to know the prayer you were speaking well enough to be able to handle the gesture without fear of losing your place. And you would want to be able to look at the water as you touched it. You would want to be able to coordinate eye, gesture, and vocal expression with ease. Furthermore, all the while you were doing this, you would not for one second want to lose awareness that you were talking with God, praying to God. Such gracefulness in expression does not happen accidentally, nor is it a product of wishful thinking and vain hope. Instead, it takes thorough preparation and practice.

As in baptism, so in communion there is great need for coordinating eye focus, gesture, and vocal expression in handling the spoken portions of the sacramental liturgy. For example, after the minister proclaims the Word through reading the Scriptures and preaching, the person serving communion typically invites the congregation to the table of the Lord using words perhaps similar to these:

> Friends, this is the joyful feast of the people of God! People will come from east and west and from north and south, and sit at table in the kingdom of God.
>
> According to Luke, when our risen Lord was at table with his disciples, he took the bread, and blessed and broke it, and gave it to them. Then their eyes were opened and they recognized him.
>
> This is the Lord's table. Our Savior invites those who trust him to share the feast he has prepared.

Now an invitation read from start to finish hardly has the feel of a personal and truly meant welcome. Rather it may seem *pro forma*. More significant, if one is tied to a book while issuing an invitation to communion such as the one given above, there is little opportunity to use eye contact and gesture at those points where such contact and gesture appear to be warranted.

When you say that people will come and "sit at table in the kingdom of God," for instance, it hardly seems natural, spontaneous, and unaffected to act as if there is nobody and no table present now at the moment of our communion! Even more particularly, when you say "This is the Lord's table," it seems at least very awkward to be staring at a book or out into space. For in the instant those words are uttered, the table is the focus of what it is you are talking about. It only makes sense, then, to look at the table and to gesture toward it. You cannot do that if you are holding on to a book for dear life with one hand while keeping your place in the book with the index finger of your other hand! Freedom is needed if an invitation is to be issued in a way that is dignified, hospitable, and truly meaningful. A thorough knowledge of what one is going to say and of what one is doing when issuing an invitation to communion consequently is necessary.

In the communion liturgy, even the Great Prayer of Thanksgiving is not spoken entirely without eye contact with the congregation, for it often is preceded with a responsive text such as this one:

> The Lord be with you.
> *And also with you.*
> Lift up your hearts.
> *We lift them to the Lord.*
> Let us give thanks to the Lord our God.
> *It is right to give our thanks and praise.*

The remarks of the person who is leading in this introduction to the eucharistic prayer—those remarks in regular, not italicized print—clearly should be spoken with direct eye focus on the congregation. And those remarks should be spoken so that the congregation actually has something to which it can respond. Otherwise the congregation's part (italicized) may come across as little more than an empty recitation of words put in people's mouths.

Nor is the Great Prayer of Thanksgiving itself necessarily read with eyes always on the text. In the version of it printed here, for example, there is at least one moment when the presider's eyes should be on the congregation. The reason for this is simply that at that moment the presider is speaking to the congregation and is asking the congregation to join with him or her in proclaiming the mystery of faith. The short passage in the prayer that is to be spoken to the congregation appears in capital letters. The rest of the presider's part in the prayer, spoken entirely without lifting the eyes from the page, is given in regular print. The congregation's lines are italicized. Try to build intensity up to those moments when the congregation speaks so that the congregation's speech is inspired, honestly motivated, and not made routine. Then, with the words, "Let us proclaim the mystery of faith," be ready to look at the people and to encourage them to join you in expressing a truly awe-filled belief.

The Great Prayer of Thanksgiving

O holy God, Father almighty, Creator of heaven and earth, with joy we give you thanks and praise.

You commanded light to shine out of darkness, divided the sea and dry land, created the vast universe and called it good. You made us in your image to live with one another in love. You gave us the breath of life and freedom to choose your way. You set forth your purpose in commandments through Moses, and called for justice in the cry of prophets. Through long generations you have been patient and kind to all your children.

How wonderful are your ways, almighty God. How marvelous is your name, O Holy One. You alone are God. Therefore with apostles and prophets, and that great cloud of witnesses who live for you beyond all time and space, we lift our hearts in joyful praise: *Holy, holy, holy Lord, God of power and might, heaven and earth are full of your glory. Hosanna in the highest. Blessed is he who comes in the name of the Lord. Hosanna in the highest.*

We praise you, most holy God, for sending your only Son Jesus to live among us, full of grace and truth. He made you known to all who received him. Sharing our joy and sorrow, he healed the sick and was a friend of sinners.

Obeying you, he took up his cross and died that we might live. We praise you that he overcame death and is risen to rule the world. He is still the friend of sinners. We trust him to overcome every power that can hurt or divide us, and believe that when he comes in glory we will celebrate victory with him.

Therefore, in remembrance of your mighty acts in Jesus Christ, we take this bread and this cup and give you praise and thanksgiving.

LET US PROCLAIM THE MYSTERY OF FAITH:

> *Christ has died,*
> *Christ is risen,*
> *Christ will come again.*

Gracious God, pour out your Holy Spirit upon us, that this bread and this cup may be for us the body and blood of our Lord, and that we, and all who share this feast, may be one with Christ and he with

us. Fill us with eternal life, that with joy we may be his faithful
people until we feast with him in glory.

Through Christ, with Christ, in Christ, in the unity of the Holy
Spirit, all glory and honor are yours, almighty [God], for ever and
ever.   *Amen.*

So far we have gone into two matters that need to be kept in
mind when administering baptism and serving communion.
First, in handling the spoken portions of these sacramental
liturgies, care must be taken to understand and express as
fully as possible the intellectual and emotional content of the
texts being spoken. Second, the texts, as they are spoken,
often call for a good deal of direct and indirect eye focus and
gesture. This means that the person administering baptism
or serving communion needs to know well everything that is
to be said so that he or she is not tied to the page. The presider
at the observance of the sacrament, that is to say, needs to be
at home with content, purpose, physical and liturgical
setting, self, and congregation. Being natural, being at ease,
will result from feeling at home with these elements. On the
other hand, it will not result from mere spontaneity, a lack of
specific preparation and trust of one's instincts in the heat of
the moment.

The third thing, and maybe the most important thing to be
said about administering baptism and serving communion,
is this: There comes a moment when the physical deed takes
precedence over speech, when bodily gesture becomes more
crucial than vocal gesture, when the action aspect of the
Word-Act of worship is stressed. In baptism that moment
obviously comes when the adult or child is baptized by
sprinkling, pouring, or immersion in the name of the triune
God. Since I have had no personal experience with
immersion, I will not presume to say anything about it.
Nevertheless, those who worship in traditions where
immersion is the norm may be able to interpret some of what
is discussed here in a way that makes the principles of
kinesics or body talk applicable to their own case.

In order to be baptized, the adult will kneel at the baptismal
font. The child may lie cradled in the arms of the minister or a
parent. The question for the person doing the baptism, in any

case, is how to get on with it. How should the baptism be carried out so that the act itself may communicate something significant about what is going on? Well, certainly the gesture, the sprinkling or pouring, cannot communicate very much if the person doing the baptism is insecure with what he or she is saying or doing. It is not that the words are hard to memorize! After all, there are not very many. The celebrant or presider simply states the given name of the individual being baptized and continues: "I baptize you in the name of the Father, and of the Son, and of the Holy Spirit."

The trouble is that the saying of the baptismal formula needs to be coordinated with the gesture of washing by sprinkling or pouring water. In some traditions, the water is applied three times as the triune God is named. That is not exactly a difficult maneuver. Most of us can manage to talk and scoop water at the same time. But where are the eyes of the person doing the baptizing focused? Sometimes I have seen them focused exclusively on the individual being baptized as if the taking of the water and sprinkling it or pouring it were almost an afterthought. At other times I have seen the eyes of the person doing the baptizing focused on the water while the name of the individual being baptized is pronounced. The individual was turned away from, that is to say, before she or he was given due recognition.

The point is that when the name of the person being baptized is spoken, that person should be looked at. Likewise, when it is time to apply the water of baptism, that symbol of cleansing should be given attention. The celebrant should turn to the baptismal font, scoop up the water deliberately, turn again to the individual being baptized, and pour or sprinkle the water while saying, "I baptize you in the name of the Father." After that the celebrant again turns to the font, scoops up the water, turns back to the person being baptized, pours or sprinkles the water, and says, "and of the Son." So also once more the same sequence of actions is undertaken, culminating in the application of the water to the person being baptized as the words "and the Holy Spirit" are spoken.

The principle is this: that the eyes are focused on the object of attention or the action being undertaken in a given moment and nothing is rushed, nothing is made perfunctory. Don't hurry. Don't be afraid to let the action at times speak for itself. And don't be afraid of drawing attention to the fact that a washing is taking place, that a ritual cleansing is occurring. After all, the water is to be heard, seen, and in the case of the person being baptized, felt. It should be clear that something is being done to him or her and that that something involves getting wet. God's grace can be just that tactile. We have notions of it, certainly. But before any of those notions, before even the word *grace* itself could be spoken by us, there was something done to us, something that could be felt. Baptism reminds us of that.

When it comes to the celebration of communion, the place where action is highlighted plainly is where the bread is broken by the person presiding at table, where the cup of the new covenant is poured out and offered, and where the people receive the elements—take and eat the bread, and drink the wine. Of course, in this book we are not focusing on the congregation's activity, but rather on the activity of the person leading in worship. Therefore we will discuss only the fraction or breaking of the bread and the offering of the cup by the presider.

As with baptism, so also with communion, the word needs to be suited to the action and the action to the word. And there needs to be freedom from any dependence on the printed page so that the eyes of the person serving communion can be focused appropriately on what he or she is doing and on those for whom it is being done. Nothing could look more outlandish than for the presider to be glancing at a worship-book text as if it were a cookbook, while handling the elements of the eucharist! Just before taking the bread, the eyes of the presider should focus on the bread. Then the bread is taken, broken, and offered to the congregation.

In that gesture of offering the bread, in reaching out with it toward those gathered at the Lord's table, keep these principles of kinesics or body language in mind: First, eye contact must precede the gesture. That is to say, the presider looks up, at, and around the congregation. The gesture of reaching out with the two halves of the loaf follows instantly upon that eye contact. The contact is made first. The gesture follows it.

Second, the range of eye contact must exceed the range of the gesture. To put it another way, one must "reach out" farther with eye contact than with gesture, or the gesture will seem exaggerated, awkward, ill-suited to the thought being expressed. In brief, the size of the gesture, the extension and width of it, will seem to exceed the size of the thought. As a result, the gesture will not be fully convincing. The reason for this is that the listener's mind goes where the speaker's eye goes. The sweep, focus, and dimension of a thought suggested through eye contact thus needs to precede and exceed any gesture with the arms and hands if that gesture is to be validated, vindicated, justified in the mind of the listener.

Third, the range of eye focus and of gesture must reach, but not exceed the perimeters of the actual congregation. One does not reach out with eye contact or gesture past the dozen or so persons huddled up front in the center pews of the sanctuary on a snowy day when most of the congregation could not get to church, as if dozens upon dozens of other persons were filling the side pews, the balcony, and the transepts. Likewise, if the balcony and transepts are full, one does not reach out with eye contact and gesture offering the bread of life only to those seated in the center pews.

Fourth, the farther the range of eye contact and the more sweeping and extended the gesture, the more elevated and expansive the presider's center must appear to be. If the center does not come alive to the demand created by the size or dimension of the thought being expressed through eye contact and gesture, the presider herself or himself may seem oddly detached from what is going on. The self may appear to be withheld from the action, almost as if to say: "Here is the bread of life. You take it, I don't want it."

When pouring and offering the cup, the same principles of kinesics or body talk apply. If one is saying, "In the same way, the Lord Jesus took the cup, after supper," one needs actually to look at the cup or chalice just before picking it up. And if one is pouring wine into the cup from a pitcher, it is important to complete that action without feeling hurried before going on to do or say anything else. Let the action itself carry its freight of meaning for people. Let them see and hear the wine poured out for them. And let them call to mind how the life of Christ was poured out for them, how, indeed, it is poured out for them now as the Spirit of Christ in the church continues to slake the thirst for God. Then go on to reach out with the cup to the people speaking words such as these: "And, having given thanks, as has been done in his name, he gave it to his disciples, saying, 'This cup' "—and here again look at the cup—" 'is the new covenant in my blood. Drink of it, all of you.' " In other words, when you refer to the cup, look at the cup briefly before resuming eye contact with those to whom you are speaking.

In sum, be a host at table in the name of the Christ who has spread his table for his people in order that they might be nourished with life eternal in the midst of the temporal life they have been called on to lead. For that temporal life, that life in time, in *this* time, in this present age is not an easy one. It is a difficult one. It is a demanding one. It is a life filled with ambiguity, discomfort, sometimes perhaps even danger and pain.

A life that witnesses to the rule of God, that anticipates the familial fellowship of the kingdom of heaven, inevitably is a life with a cross in it. It is a life troubled with things as they are. It is a life *in* trouble with a world seemingly bent on having its "haves" and "have-nots," its insiders and outsiders, its own way and not God's way. A life that witnesses to the rule of God is a life resonant with the life of Christ, and so it is cruciform, joyously so, for Christ is victor. Yet a life that witnesses to the rule of God is sober, too, for the victory of Christ is not yet manifest everywhere in everything. It is not yet manifest in the church. It is not yet manifest in you and me.

And this brings me to what I would like to say in concluding this book on effective speech communication in leading worship: Our task in developing competence as worship leaders is not complete, nor will our task be complete until the life represented in our worship, proclaimed in the reading of the Scriptures and preaching, and celebrated in the sacraments, is perfected by God's grace in God's time. Consequently, though we strive to improve our understanding of what we are about and how best to be about it, we do not panic over blunders, inadequacies, or our lack of consummate ability, for we are not called to be consummate. We are called to be faithful, that is, trusting and diligent.

It has been said that if you understood communion, you would not need it. It might also be said, I think, that if we could become consummate in worship, nobody would need worship—or those of us who lead worship! For the *parousia* would have come upon us, the kingdoms of this world would have become the kingdom of our Lord and of our Lord's Christ, and our lives and the life of the church and world would have been brought into *shalom*, the just, full-orbed peace of God.

That obviously has not yet happened. So, instead of possessing the future, we live as those possessed by it. And we assess our efforts, not in relation to what we ourselves or others have achieved, but in relation to our mutual goal. We are colleagues in leading worship. Therefore we inspire, guide, support, and challenge one another, as we are inspired, guided, supported, and challenged by those we serve, our sisters and brothers in Christ, the church. In leading worship as in all else, then, we pray that that Spirit of counsel and might given in Christ's name to the church may take us as we are and press us into the service of what God would have us be. And to God alone be the praise and the glory, always and ever. Amen.

BIBLIOGRAPHY

INTERPRETATIVE SPEECH TEXTS

Bacon, Wallace A. *The Art of Interpretation*. New York: Holt, Rinehart & Winston, 1972.

Bartow, Charles L. *The Preaching Moment*. Nashville: Abingdon, 1980. (Although the title says "preaching," the book has much to say about interpretative speech, voice, diction, and kinesics or body language that is applicable to leading worship.)

Beloof, Robert. *The Performing Voice in Literature*. Boston: Little, Brown & Co., 1966.

Bozarth-Campbell, Alla. *The Word's Body*. University: University of Alabama Press, 1979.

Geiger, Don. *The Sound, Sense and Performance of Literature*. Chicago: Scott, Foresman & Co., 1963.

Lamar, Nedra Newkirk. *How to Speak the Written Word*. Westwood, N.J.: Fleming H. Revell Co., 1949.

Lee, Charlotte I. *Oral Interpretation*. Boston: Houghton Mifflin, 1971.
————. *Oral Reading of the Scriptures*. Boston: Houghton Mifflin, 1974.

Long, Beverly Whitaker, and Mary Frances HopKins. *Literature in Performance*. Englewood Cliffs, N.J.: Prentice-Hall, 1982.

TEXTS ON WORSHIP AND THE SACRAMENTS

Baillie, Donald M. *The Theology of the Sacraments*. New York: Charles Scribner's Sons, 1957.

Burkhart, John E. *Worship: A Searching Examination of the Liturgical Experience*. Philadelphia: Westminster Press, 1982.

Hovda, Robert. *Strong, Loving and Wise: Presiding in Liturgy*. Washington: Liturgical Conference, 1976.

Macleod, Donald. *Presbyterian Worship*. Atlanta: John Knox Press, 1980.

Nichols, J. Randall. *The Restoring Word*. San Francisco: Harper & Row, Publishers, 1987. (Although Dr. Nichols' book is on pastoral preaching, chapter 7 is on the worship environment and resonates well with themes in this book.)

Old, Hughes Oliphant. *Worship*. Atlanta: John Knox Press, 1984.

Stookey, Lawrence Hull. *Baptism: Christ's Act in the Church*. Nashville: Abingdon, 1982.

White, James F. *Christian Worship in Transition*. Nashville: Abingdon, 1976.

———. *Introduction to Christian Worship*. Nashville: Abingdon, 1980.

Willimon, William H. *Worship as Pastoral Care*. Nashville: Abingdon, 1979.

SOURCES OF LITURGICAL TEXTS USED IN THIS BOOK

The Book of Common Prayer. New York: Seabury Press, 1973.

The Book of Common Worship. Philadelphia: The Presbyterian Church in the United States of America, 1946.

Holy Baptism and Services for the Renewal of Baptism. Philadelphia: Westminster Press, 1985.

The Service for the Lord's Day. Philadelphia: Westminster Press, 1984.

INDEX

Absolution, 19
Altar, 25
Anamnesis, 24
Apostles' Creed, 43, 115
Attitude, 86, 91-94, 95, 97, 99, 101, 102, 104, 111, 112, 113
Augustine, 108

Baptism, 54, 108, 111, 114, 115, 116, 119, 120
Barr, Browne, 26
Beeners, W. J., 47, 76
Benediction, 28, 32, 55-56, 85, 108
Book of Common Prayer, 82
Breath control, 39, 40, 41
Browning, Robert, 23

Call to worship, 25, 27, 28, 32, 55-66, 85, 108; responsive, 62
Calvin, John, 108, 109
Catechetical preaching, 81
Choir, 23, 67, 76, 81, 82
Christian year, 57, 75
Church, 16, 17, 21, 56, 57, 65, 69, 75, 88, 110, 122, 123, 124; Body of Christ, 89; ecumenical, 17-18; local, 18
Clergy, 57
Climax, 41, 66, 99, 112
Communion, 15, 16, 18, 54, 108, 112, 116, 119, 121, 124; elements of, 108, 114, 121; table, 25, 114, 116, 121, 123
Communion of saints, 109
Confession, 25, 32, 67-75, 81, 85
Connecting words, 36, 37, 39

Declaration of pardon, 67, 69, 71, 72
Denouement, 112
Diction, 26
Divine initiative in worship, 16, 21, 23, 24, 55, 58
Divine Presence in worship, 55, 56, 62, 63
Drama, 24, 25
Dramatic action, 36, 39

Ecumenical awareness in worship, 17, 58
Effective speech, 14, 21, 31, 103, 108, 113, 123

Embodiment, 24, 92, 108, 111
Empathic response, 92
Empathy, 24, 102
Emphasis, 32, 42-54, 65, 72, 79, 111; means of, 44-51, 54
Epic voice, 98
Epistle lesson, 75, 80, 89, 94, 105
Erasmus, 108
Eucharist, 16, 108, 114, 121
Expression, 31, 88, 103, 116
Eye contact, 61, 103, 113, 114, 116, 121-23; direct, 103, 105, 106, 114, 117, 119; indirect, 103, 105, 106, 119; principles of, 103-5

Facial expression, 26, 63, 65, 91, 92, 103, 113, 115
Feedback, 65
Forgiveness, 20, 70
Fraction, 121

Gesture, 26, 63, 64, 65, 102, 108, 109, 113, 115, 116, 119, 121, 122
Gospel, 17, 68
Gospel lesson, 75, 80, 89, 105
Great Prayer of Thanksgiving, 117-19

Historical sense in worship, 16, 58, 81
Hospitality, 25
Hovda, Robert, 61
Human response in worship, 16, 21, 23, 24, 25, 58
Hymnbook, 17, 57
Hymnody, 17
Hymns, 17, 23, 81

Inflection, 44, 47, 49, 50, 51, 54; circumflex, 49, 50; falling, 49, 50; rising, 49, 50
Innovation in worship, 17, 21, 23, 24
Intensity, 45
Interpretative dynamic, 25, 28, 30, 85, 87, 113
Intonational pattern, 47

Jesus Christ, 16-21, 56-59, 64, 65-69, 72, 73, 75, 85, 87, 88, 91, 108, 109, 110, 114, 115, 118, 119, 123, 124

Kinesics, 119, 121, 122
Kingdom of God, 16, 18, 19, 25, 56
Kingdom of heaven, 123
Knox, John, 108

Laity, 57
Leading worship, 14, 15, 18, 24-33, 45, 57-59, 60-65, 70, 72, 79, 80, 82, 87, 98, 103, 108, 113, 121, 123, 124
Lectionary, 15, 75
Litanies, 32
Literary context, 53, 58, 90
Liturgics, 15
Liturgist, 27
Lord's day, 15, 57, 67, 75
Lord's Prayer, 32, 67
Lord's supper, 108
Luther, Martin, 89
Lyric voice, 98

Mannerism, 26
Mozart, Wolfgang Amadeus, 23, 43

Nature of worship, 14, 16, 18
Norms of worship, 14

Offering, 23, 24
Old Testament lesson, 75, 80, 89, 105
Oral interpretation, 26
Order of worship, 23, 28, 81

Parallelism, 77, 78; antithetical, 77; climactic, 78; constructive, 77; synonymous, 77
Parenthetical expressions, 35, 36, 39
Parousia, 124
Particularity of worship, 21, 23, 24
Pause, 37, 39-41, 44, 45-47, 48, 51, 52, 54, 113
Pentecost, 105
Perception, 31
Personal significance in worship, 18, 20, 21, 23, 24
Petition, 21
Phrasing, 32-41, 54, 65, 72, 79, 86, 111
Pitch, 47, 48, 52
Point of view, 86, 94-102, 111, 112, 113
Poise, 47
Posture, 26, 65, 91, 92, 103
Potok, Chaim, 55
Praise, 21, 60, 67, 79, 81, 90, 91, 97, 108, 124
Prayer, 23, 28, 60, 61, 67, 104, 115

Prelude, 27
Processionals, 65
Psalter: reading of, 28, 32; responsive reading of, 32, 67, 75-84; unison reading of, 32, 67, 76
Public-corporate worship, 18, 19, 21, 23
Punctuation, 33, 38

Recessionals, 65
Reign of God, 56
Repentance, 69, 70
Responsive reading, 32, 81
Restitution, 20
Rule of God, 123

Sacrament, 24, 25, 75, 81, 108, 109, 111, 113, 119, 124
Sacrifice, 24
Sanctuary, 19, 22, 25, 26, 27, 63, 65, 70
Scherer, Paul, 89
Scripture, 15, 16, 21, 23, 24, 57, 58, 59, 67, 75; reading of, 28, 85-107, 108, 109, 110, 111, 116, 123
Sensory memory, 101, 102
Service of worship, 14, 18, 27, 59, 71, 75, 80, 87
Setting for worship, 26, 27, 28, 45, 58, 85, 87, 89, 106, 112, 119
Sex-inclusive language, 58, 106
Shakespeare, William, 23
Shalom, 124
Situational dynamic, 25, 28, 30, 85, 87, 113
Speaker's center, 64, 91, 112, 122
Spirit, 24, 30, 66, 68, 76, 85, 87, 88, 92, 110, 115, 123, 124
Stress, 44, 45, 47, 48, 51, 54

Tensiveness, 20, 21, 22, 23
Third-person narrator, 99
Tradition in worship, 17, 21, 23, 24
Trinity, 63

Unison reading, 32
Universality of worship, 21, 23, 24

Verbal quotation mark, 38
Vocal tone, 26
Volume, 45

Wesley, Charles, 17
Wesley, John, 17
Words of institution, 112, 113